Break Into Sports Through Ticket Sales

By
Mark Washo

ISBN: 0-9728884-0-3

Chapter Listing

Preface

So you want to work in the front office of a professional sports team? Like most candidates looking to land a job in professional sports, you probably think that you want to be in marketing, community relations, or public relations. As a hiring executive, I have heard this countless times. The problem is that marketing, public relations, and community relations are where the fewest opportunities exist. Most candidates trying to break into sports are simply looking in the wrong place.

The reality is that most job openings are in ticket sales. If you want to break into sports, you should search where the most opportunities are with the least amount of competition. Ticket sales is the backbone of many sports teams and produces a large percentage of the revenues. It is also the best way for you to get that ever-so-important "foot in the door."

Why is it that most people search for jobs in sports where the fewest opportunities exist? For starters, ticket sales gets little recognition or credit within the industry, even though it is a very important function of any team's front office.

Few colleges and universities teach about sales as a profession and virtually no one teaches about ticket sales. Even with the emergence of excellent sports management programs around the country, this problem still exists.

Instead of teaching about ticket sales, many sports management curriculums focus on the more "glamorous" sides of the sports business such as marketing, public relations, and community relations. There is no question these disciplines are important and there is an obligation to teach a well-rounded curriculum when it comes to sports marketing. However, as good as some of these programs are, most fail to teach in depth about ticket sales.

Another issue is that as great as the opportunities are within ticket sales, it is still a career that has somewhat of a negative perception. There are those who feel that ticket sales is only an entry-level position and that selling is "beneath them." Many people base this on what they perceive to be some of the less-appealing aspects of ticket sales such as having to make cold calls, dealing with rejections, and overcoming objections. These perceptions exist; however, most are based on a lack of understanding of what sales is really all about.

I have been fortunate enough to have a career in professional sports for the past twelve years, first working for AAA minor league baseball, then the National Basketball Association, and most recently as vice president of ticket sales for a Major League Soccer team. My entire sports career to this point has been in ticket sales. Ticket sales has been a tremendously rewarding career for me. It is one that I am passionate about and a job that many people envy. I have heard countless times, "Wow, what a great job you have working for a professional sports team. It must be wonderful being in a job you love"—and it's true!

Ticket sales is a great way to begin a career in professional sports. I personally have been successful selling tickets and I can teach others how to have similar success. Following simple steps for sales success will lead those with the right characteristics to be successful.

Many people have personality characteristics and traits that would make them good ticket sales professionals. However, they don't know it. Recognizing that your traits and characteristics match up with other successful sales professionals in the industry can help you consider ticket sales as the right way for you to get your career started.

I wish I had learned early on in college that I had the tools to be a good sales professional. Because of my personality traits, ticket sales would be the way I could break into sports.

Make no mistake about it: ticket sales is an extremely tough profession, especially in the beginning when you are building your client base. This job is not for everyone. It requires strong personality characteristics and an ability to look past some of the negative aspects of sales that make it a profession of which many people are afraid. Most of these "fears," however, are based more on the perceived negative aspects of sales rather than the actual truth.

The bottom line is that professional sports teams are relying more and more on revenues generated from tickets sales. Attendance is slipping in just about every major professional sport, including the almighty National Football League. Knowing how to sell tickets will be an extremely beneficial talent now and into the future.

If you love professional sports and are interested in the business of sports from a sales and marketing perspective, then this book is for you. Most sports business books focus on the side of the business as it relates to player trades, salary caps, and building championship teams. This book will not touch on any of those subjects. This book will explain how to get the job to sell tickets and fill stadiums. Reading this may give you a different perspective on some of the behind-the-scenes business matters that are found in the sports industry. It will make you think about professional sports differently than you currently do.

Behind every seat sold and corporate box filled, there are marketing plans, sales strategies, and PR initiatives making attendance happen. Regardless of the sports career position that you chose, the facts contained here will help you gain a better understanding of the type of opportunities that exist in the industry. Regardless of what you currently think about ticket sales now, you should read this book with an open mind. If you want to learn more about the business aspects of professional sports, read on. But most importantly, if you want to break into professional sports and think you have what it takes to succeed in ticket sales, read on, and break into sports!

CHAPTER 1

The Current Climate of Professional Sports: Declining Attendance

The current climate of professional sports in the United States is changing. Almost all professional sports teams are facing the same issue, declining attendance. Season tickets, group sales, and walk-up ticket sales are all down with most leagues and teams.

The next time you watch a Major League Baseball game on television, notice what the advertising boards behind home plate read. Chances are you will see a sign that reads, "For Tickets Call . . ." or "For Group Sales Call . . ." Why would teams advertise for ticket sales on a sign that is their most lucrative signage location in the stadium? It is because these teams *need* to sell more tickets!

A Decline in Attendance

I do not want to paint a gloom-and-doom scenario for all professional sports. Many teams are doing well at the gate and are packing in stadiums and selling a lot of tickets. However, as I began researching sports attendance, I found a greater number of articles supporting the fact that attendance is slipping than I thought I would. According to recent headlines in the *Sports Business Journal*, most, if not all, sports leagues are experiencing a decline in attendance.

National Football League (NFL)

[The] **NFL's Miami Dolphins, having failed to sell out last season's home playoff game in time to avoid a local television blackout, have changed their playoff ticket sales policies.** Under a new initiative, Dolphin season ticket holders would get $8 to $18 dollar discounts off the individual game prices for a wild card or divisional playoff match-up and $11 to $25 discounts off the individual game prices for the AFC Championship game. The Dolphins are the first NFL team to create such a policy. (*Sports Business Journal*, December 2-8, 2002)

Players join ticket-renewal drive. The Saints this week will send 2,000 letters signed by individual players to 2002 season-ticket holders who have yet to renew their seats. The move is the latest by major professional team facing a tough economy and declining attendance that enlists players and coaches to woo fans. (*Sports Business Journal*, March 24-30, 2003)

NFL teams hustle in attempt to avoid blackout blues. Teams are looking for local companies to guarantee ticket sales in an effort to avoid the NFL's local blackout rule. Four teams, the Oakland Raiders, Arizona Cardinals, Jacksonville Jaguars, and the Indianapolis Colts had their games blacked out in the second weekend of the 2003 NFL season. This followed one blackout, in Seattle during the first weekend. (*Sports Business Journal*, September 22-28, 2003)

Major League Baseball (MLB)

Last season's attendance drop (in Major League Baseball) was the second straight decline and the largest dip since 1996. Fewer fans watched twenty-four of the thirty teams. The Milwaukee Brewers experienced the largest drop at 30 percent. (*Sports Business Journal*, December 9-15, 2002)

New ballparks sport old look: Empty seats. Whether it's because of poor weather, a lousy economy, a rebuilding process that has delivered a weak product in many of the newer parks, or all of the above, MLB attendance declined 4.2 percent for the first quarter of the season, continuing a downturn that began last year. (*Sports Business Journal*, December 9-15, 2003)

Indians to try variable ticket pricing as season ticket sales slump. Tribe seeks to boost revenue with higher prices for marquee games. The year brought the third consecutive season of decline at the gate for a club that sold out 455 games in a row between June 7, 1995, and April 2, 2001. (*Sports Business Journal*, October 14-20, 2003)

Marlins still fishing for fans. There are tough sells, and then there's the daily task facing Florida Marlins executives, who must feel more and more like ice salesmen in an Eskimo village. Five months after the club rode an old manager and a few young stars to an improbable World Series title over the Yankees, the story of the year in baseball has brought a mere 2500 new season ticket holders and little political support for a new stadium. (*Sports Business Journal*, April 5-11, 2004)

National Basketball Association (NBA)

After the team sold every seat for ten seasons, the Charlotte Hornets attendance last season plummeted to 10,623 fans a night. (*Sports Business Journal*, February 25-March 3, 2002)

The Phoenix Suns have rolled out an aggressive ticket-marketing campaign to reverse last season's 9 percent decline in attendance. (*Sports Business Journal*, September 2-8, 2003)

NBA season tickets fall but gate climbs. The NBA is suffering this season from an overall decline in season ticket sales, according to a confidential league report, but savvy marketing efforts have in resulted in an increase in total attendance. The reports show an 8 percent drop in season ticket sales across the teams. It also showed a 4 percent decline in season-ticket renewals. (*Sports Business Journal*, February 17-23, 2002)

League attendance dips 0.5 percent. The NBA saw its total announced attendance for the regular season edge downward this year as the league was unable to overcome a setback in season ticket sales. (*Sports Business Journal*, April 21-27, 2003)

Knicks look outside for ticket sales spark. With a drop in season ticket sales and a less-than-sold-out Madison Square Garden, the team is now turning to its corporate partners to help brand the franchise. (*Sports Business Journal*, December 8-14, 2003)

National Hockey League (NHL)

Panthers beef up sales staff despite labor uncertainty. With the threat of a lockout hanging over the NHL, the Florida Panthers have decided to adjust the size of their staff. They're hiring more people. The Club plans to bring in an additional 20 sales people over the next few months, in addition to the 25 new hires made since the fall. (*Sports Business Journal*, April 19-25, 2004)

Because professional sports teams are having a difficult time selling tickets through traditional methods, there is a growing opportunity for people who know how to sell. Teams can no longer simply hang a "For Sale" sign in the window and expect people to come to games. They need to do much more than place ads in the weekend sports page.

As further evidence that ticket sales is the way to get your career started in sports, this headline was taken from a Career in Sports Seminar article.

> **Students with no desire to be salespeople have no business being in the sports business.**

That is what seven sports industry professionals stressed to students during a panel discussion, Careers in Sports, yesterday in the Executive Seminar Room in the Lender School of Business Center. Quinnipiac's Office of Career Services sponsored the program.

"Sports is a business of sales," said Christopher Canetti '92, vice president of marketing for Major League Soccer's New York/New Jersey MetroStars. "Our job is to sell."

The owner and general manager of the Bridgeport Bluefish baseball team said he spends more time marketing than dealing with baseball issues. "Our business is about how many people we can attract," he said. (*QU Daily*, November 17, 2003)

So What's the Solution to the Decline in Attendance?
Are New Stadiums the Answer?

Brand-new stadiums won't solve the declining attendance problem, although many sports executives, cities, and leagues thought this was the answer. Brand-new stadiums, arenas, and venues are springing up in major cities across the country with the hopes of selling more tickets and increasing revenues. Teams with new stadiums do indeed experience ticket sales growth the first several years. However, once the novelty of a new stadium begins to wear off, attendance again begins to decline.

Examples of this situation can be seen in cities such as Buffalo, Cleveland, Denver, Charlotte, and Pittsburgh. The list goes on and professional sports owners are now realizing that the old saying "build it and they will come" is no longer necessarily true. This has consequently made securing new financing deals with cities increasingly difficult.

How About Owning a Popular Sports Team?

Of course there are exceptions to the rule and there are still sports franchises that are doing extremely well. Teams that have tradition and heritage on their side are still selling a lot of tickets. The New York Yankees, for example, continue to pull in record crowds. They have been a perennial powerhouse on the field and have over 100 years of baseball nostalgia as part of their history. They have also been synonymous with the city of New York and are a major tourist attraction for visitors from all over the world. Other teams such as the Chicago Cubs and Boston Red Sox are also in this category.

However, even teams that fall in this category still need ticket sales help. The Yankees and Red Sox have ticket sales forces to help keep attendance strong and offer group discounts, mini plans, and special ticket promotions, all which must be sold. Even the popular NFL who traditionally never had a ticket sales force is now hiring corporate and group sales representatives to help fill their stadiums.

How About a Winning Team?

Even winning doesn't guarantee sellouts, another myth that doesn't necessarily hold true in the professional sports world as much as it used to. Many owners used to claim that "start winning and people will come."

Although of course, there is usually a spike in attendance and sellouts for teams that experience success on the field or advance far into the postseason, this attendance spike typically has a short life. It also does not translate into the next season and has a minimal impact on new-season ticket sales the following year. Examples of this can be seen for teams such as the Florida Marlins, the Washington Capitals, and the New Jersey Nets. All of these teams experienced great spikes in attendance during championship runs. However, increases in attendance were only slight in subsequent seasons and did not translate into major increases in season ticket sales.

The Florida Marlins attendance plummeted so far after their 1991 championship season that Marlins games were the least attended games in all of the teams in Major League Baseball. Once the hottest ticket in town, Marlins tickets were found in every dumpster in the city. This all changed, of course, during the 2003 season when they made another World Series appearance. However, if the Marlins follow suit like many other teams, this championship run will not impact ticket sales as much as they would like in subsequent seasons.

More Examples of Attendance Struggles

Further evidence of declining attendance can be seen with the following examples from the Toronto Blue Jay's and the New Knicks.

Toronto Blue Jays

In 1991 while I was at Bison Baseball, I recall sitting through a presentation about ticket sales by the Toronto Blue Jays organization. Their executives told us the Sky Dome was sold out *every* regular season home game with season tickets. Even more impressive, they said they had a 10,000-person waiting list for new season tickets. Now, a little more than 10 years later, it appears there is no longer a waiting list. In fact, a quick trip to their Web site will show you that season tickets are available in just about every seating area in the stadium.

New York Knicks

In the fall of 2002, NBA's mighty New York Knicks sent a letter to their 10,000-person season ticket waiting list announcing that they had 2,000 season tickets available. For the first time in the *history* of the organization, the Knicks had to go public with the fact that they had season tickets available.

They called through their entire 10,000-person waiting list and still did not sell the 2,000 available tickets. For the first time Madison Square Garden was not sold out with season tickets. They had their first "non-sellout" game in the history of the franchise during one of their early season games and subsequently had to introduce mini plans for the first time. They went as far as to credit a "brilliant" ticket advertising campaign developed by an expensive sports marketing firm to help sell less than 2,000 tickets to a 10,000-person waiting list.

This ad agency created a revolutionary advertisement that stated something like, "The Knicks are Your Team, NYC—Buy Tickets." Soon, even the New York Knicks may have to staff and create a ticket sales department.

So What "IS" the Solution to the Problem?

The solution to the problem is a complex one and cannot be answered easily.

However, recruiting and hiring a professional ticket sales force is one of them. Today, just about all of the sports leagues and teams in the country recruit and hire ticket sales professionals.

According to my research, the Jacksonville Jaguars were one of the first NFL teams to introduce a group sales ticket department to an NFL front office. NFL teams never before had to have a proactive group sales department because the teams simply sold tickets through their box office and not through a sales office.

The NFL traditionally had such great demand for their tickets that a larger percentage of their stadiums were sold in season ticket packages. However, the Jaguars did not sell out their stadium with season tickets and came to the conclusion they needed a group sales department to help sell out their stadium. I recall attending a Sports Marketing Conference in Boston back in the late 1990s and remember being impressed by the fact that the Jaguars had an aggressive group ticket sales department. They had great programs, and were the only NFL team at the conference representing ticket sales.

Many other NFL teams have followed suit, adding group ticket sales and corporate ticket sales departments. The NFL is now on the same page with other professional sports teams who rely on ticket sales professionals.

Welcome to the world of professional ticket sales Toronto Blue Jays, Jacksonville Jaguars, and the New York Knicks—and welcome to *your* opportunity to break into a professional sports. Remember, major league sports teams around the country are experiencing a decline in attendance. **They need you!**

CHAPTER 2

Ticket Sales: What's the Problem?

Although there is no simple answer as to why attendance is down for many sports teams, there are several contributing factors. These factors are some of the problems and challenges that many sports leagues are facing today. Once again, this is not to say that all professional sports are in trouble; however, the following issues are some of the reasons why attendance is slipping.

Time Conflicts

People lead extremely busy lives. Between work, family obligations, and extra-curricular activities, people have less time to spend on leisure activities such as attending professional sporting events. Those with children have even less time. When someone decides to give up several hours on a weeknight or a weekend to attend a four-hour professional sporting event, they make a significant time commitment. Attending a game becomes one more thing that must be fit into an already busy schedule.

Competition for professional sports teams expands beyond just the other sports teams in a marketplace. Teams face competition from all other recreational and leisure activities available in the area. In New York City for example, not only must a sports franchise compete against the seven area professional teams, they must also compete with the Jersey shore, the Hamptons, parks, boating, biking, Broadway shows, tourist attractions, and just about every other leisure activity imaginable. There are endless entertainment options from which to choose.

High Costs

Contributing as well to the decline in attendance is the growing cost of attending a game. Let's assume that a conservative estimate on the average professional sports ticket is $40. This means that a family of four attending a professional sports game must pay $160 just for the game tickets. Now add $10 to park the car, $5 for a beer, $3 for each soft drink, $4 for a hot dog, $30 for a team souvenir, and this can quickly turn into a $200-plus outing. Think of everything else a family can do with $200. Especially during a weak economy, people begin to think about how much they are spending and where they are spending their entertainment dollars.

Negative Image of Athletes and Inflated Salaries

Another problem plaguing professional sports is the growing negative image of professional athletes. Some athletes think they are above signing autographs, going to player appearances, and being accessible to fans. Thus, more and more fans begin to question why they should support overpaid athletes who simply do not care about them.

This negative perception is worsened by some of the off-field problems faced by many pro athletes. Stories concerning athletes who have gotten into trouble with the law for violence, drugs, domestic abuse, and sex scandals always make it to the top of sports news coverage. Look at the coverage that athletes such as O.J. Simpson and Kobe Bryant have received. The media coverage surrounding these athletes is unprecedented in sports history. Add to this, the inflation of player salaries as compared to the salaries of the average fan. Think for a minute about the average salary of the fan sitting in the stadium compared to the average salary of an athlete playing in the game. The gap is quite astounding. Over time, fans have become frustrated about paying exorbitant ticket prices to watch overpaid athletes who don't appear to care about them and who get in trouble with the law.

Player Trades and Free Agency

Additional factors contributing to the decline in attendance are the recent influx of player trades and the free-agency movement. Fans become emotionally connected not only to a team, but also to its star players. It is difficult for a fan to repeatedly have a favorite player traded to another team or leave due to free agency.

Sports fans find it extremely irritating when their favorite player who they have been rooting for over a number of years suddenly leaves for another team. This is especially upsetting when the player goes to a team they hate. Fans get frustrated and may no longer go to games.

Lack of Customer Service

Attendance problems are compounded even further by an overall lack of attention to customer service from both the teams' front offices as well as the team venues. Many of America's professional sports venues are run with an operational-minded attitude, in part due to necessity to ensure fan safety. With tens of thousands of fans coming into a stadium, stadium operations are the No. 1 priority.

Stadium operations are concerned with security, crowd control, ticket takers, ushers, and concessionaires. They are very important in ensuring a large volume of fans get into the stadium, find their seats, and are able to attend the game in a safe environment—a critical aspect of putting on a game. However, many stadiums pay too much attention to stadium operations to the detriment of customer service.

The problem occurs when sports venues take a heavy stadium focus too far. In some sports venues, fans are perceived as a nuisance rather than customers and the reason the organization is in business. Stadium employees treat fans as if they should feel privileged to walk the "sacred" grounds of their stadiums. They simply do not practice customer service and over time fans notice.

It is, of course, difficult trying to control a mass of people and still retain customer service. It is similar to trying to keep quality control on an assembly line. The more volume on the assembly line, the more difficult it is to maintain high quality control. However, good companies find a way to churn out a high volume of products yet keep a high level of quality. Disney theme parks, for example, have tens of thousands of people walking through their gates on a daily basis, yet their attention to customer service is impeccable.

This lack of customer service often extends to some of the front office staff as well. Many teams only communicate with their fans when it is time to renew ticket packages. Therefore, instead of maintaining a relationship throughout the season, the only time a season ticket holder hears from someone in the front office is when it is time for the team to ask for money. This in turn may lead to frustrated fans who feel taken advantage of.

The lack of customer service also applies to the stadium box office. Many professional teams' front offices rely on box office personnel with a lack of business experience to handle customer service. These employees are often overworked and understaffed. Some only work on game days and because they do not work in the front office on a day-to-day basis may not understand some of the ticket issues. Teams have also been spoiled by a high demand for their product and often hire employees who are simply fans of the teams themselves. Therefore, these employees also focus more on operations than customer service.

Some employees become arrogant about being an employee of a team and feel they are above the average fan. They feel privileged to wear an "all access" credential badge, allowing them to walk around the stadium and even onto the field. This feeling of superiority to the fan often extends to how they treat their customers.

Unfortunately, high demand for a product often equates to poor customer service. This extends beyond the professional sports world as well. In situations where high demand exists for a product, companies can lose sight of quality customer service. The most successful companies pay attention to customer service at all times.

If fans repeatedly are treated poorly at games, they begin to feel like a number instead of a paying customer. Repeated poor customer service begins to wear on fans and eventually negative experiences add up. Average sports fans begin asking themselves if it is really worth going to professional sporting events, only to receive poor customer service.

Emotional Attachment

The concept of poor customer service brings us to another issue: emotional attachment to a team. The reason most fans are able to endure all of the things just mentioned—from high-ticket prices to unacceptable customer service—is because true fans have an emotional attachment to their team. They feel as if they have a stake in the ultimate performance of the team; they honestly care if their team wins or loses and need to be there to support their team through thick and thin.

However, if the fans begin to feel taken advantage of, they may become disenchanted with the team—and if a team constantly loses, frustration builds up. When a fan is emotionally attached to a team, while it is positive in one regard, it can also backfire and turn the fan away from a team. One small customer service mistake, one rude comment made by a stadium usher, or one arrogant employee could be the final breaking point to push the ticket holder over the edge and quit being a fan. Combine poor customer service with a losing team, and one can see how teams can lose fans.

Catering to the Corporate Dollar

This leads us to the final problem with professional sports these days. Too many teams cater to the corporate entertainment dollar—the corporate fans—and not enough to the "Average-Joe" fan. Take a look around the next time you are at professional sports venue. Who has all the good seats, luxury suites, or club seats? It sure isn't the guy who has on the team jersey, cap, and crazy boxer shorts. It is the big shot CEO sitting with the corporate clients, eating shrimp cocktail and wining and dining the company's customers.

A small-business owner once told me a story, which relates to the topic of teams catering to the corporate dollar. For many years, this particular small-business owner held season tickets to a sports team in the New York City area. One year, he received a renewal invoice that reflected a significant price increase. Upset with the increase, the small-business owner called his sales representative to complain he was no longer able to afford to buy full-season tickets. He was, however, willing to downgrade to a half-season plan because he loved his seats and was a big fan of the team.

The sales rep informed him that his particular seat location was reserved for full-season tickets only and that, in accordance with team policy, if he wanted to go with the half-season plan, he would have to move to the corner locations of the venue or the upper deck. Unhappy with this policy, the small-business owner cancelled his tickets and asked to speak to the president of the team. When he did not hear from the president after several days, he decided that was the last penny this particular team would ever get from him. While he was still a fan of the team, he would rather watch games on television.

Eventually the team president did return his call but defended the policy and price increase by explaining that their team had a great season and as a result raised their prices to cover growing costs to retain the players who had made it a successful year. When the small-business owner tried to explain his financial constraints and how he still wanted to support the team with a half-season plan with the same seats, the president responded that although he appreciated the fact that the businessman had been a loyal season ticket holder, there were corporate clients lining up to get those seats.

That pretty much did it for our friend, the small-business owner. As of that conversation, true to his word, the guy stopped going to games and even stopped watching the games on television. And as a result of that conversation, he stopped being a fan altogether.

Here is where this team president made a mistake. There are certainly times when you resign yourself to the fact that not all fans will be happy with price increases or changes in policy. However, there are always exceptions to the rule. In this particular instance, the team president should have told this guy that because of his loyalty to the team, he would make a one-year exception to the policy. He could have then sold the half-season ticket to the small-business owner and the other half to someone else with the expectation that next season the small-business owner would upgrade to full-season tickets.

Whether the team actually had companies lined up to buy these seats is almost irrelevant to the story (although I doubt that they actually had companies lining up to buy tickets for those seats), because what they lost was more important. For starters, they would have had more than the full-ticket revenue from the two half-season ticket sales (typically half-season plans are more expensive per ticket than full-season tickets), but that's not all they lost. They lost the revenue not only from this season, but also from future seasons.

Let's say for simplicity's sake that the half-season tickets cost $500 each, resulting in a $1,000 sale. If the small-business owner decided to upgrade back to full-season tickets the following season at $1,000 and continue to do so for five years, over time that would equate to $5,000 of ticket revenue for the team. Therefore, if they found a way to retain the small-business owner, plus sell the company that had been waiting in line, they would have captured business from both parties for the team.

Instead, not only did they lose the revenue from the ticket sale but just as importantly, they lost a fan who was emotionally connected to their team; a fan who would have been there through thick and thin supporting the team; a fan who would buy merchandise, visit the Web site, and attend playoff games and pep rallies. They may have gained a corporate client, but the risk they take is that the minute the company decides to cut spending, season tickets will be the first to go.

The corporate dollar is extremely important to a professional sports team. However, those attending the game in the luxury suites are often there for different reasons than true fans who support the team. Those in suites care more if they cut the next business deal than if the team wins or loses. Thus the team experiences the problem: Many teams have catered to the corporate "fan" to the detriment of the average fan; the fans who will typically be there through winning seasons and losing seasons. The corporate fan will be there if the economy is good and if they have additional entertainment dollars in their budgets.

More teams simply need to find a way to cater to both. The corporate dollar is important because their spending budgets are obviously a great deal higher than the individual's budget. However, teams need to build their fan bases with the average fan in mind—someone who will have an emotional attachment to the sport and team. These are the people who will be there for the team and who will spend the money in its support.

Fans will say things like, "I had to be there for that game," or "There is no way I was going to miss that game," or "I drove all night to get there for the game on the road." These fans are precious and teams need to nurture more like these by catering to them.

A Hard Lesson Learned About the New Era in Sports

Before leaving the subject, I thought it would be valuable to share one last example of why teams are having trouble selling tickets and thus providing the growing opportunity for people who know how to sell. In 2002, I interviewed with the newest minor league in the United States, the National Basketball Development League (NBDL). The reason I am mentioning this interview is for the simple reason that this league blew it in the first year of their launch.

The NBDL is the NBA's version of Minor League Baseball and is trying to establish a minor league to support the NBA in the way of player, coach, and front-office staff development. During their launch in 2002, eight markets were chosen in the South. They entered these markets with the idea "Here comes the NBA, we are coming to your town!"

They proceeded to hire operational-driven team presidents to set up the operational aspects of the team and focused on areas such as hiring public relations directors, player development directors, game-day operations directors, box office managers, accountants, and team administrators. They failed to hire "true" sales and marketing professionals who could create a sales and marketing culture within their organizations.

This is where they went wrong and why they are quickly learning a lesson from their mistake. The NBDL went into these markets thinking that they would automatically have demand for their product because they were the NBA. They approached the market with traditional local market advertising such as billboards, radio and newspaper advertising. Then they opened the doors. Their stadium operations were perfectly in place, they had all the aspects of running a league and teams down to a science—the NBA way. They thought they were ready for their first season to begin.

The big problem was that when they opened the doors, guess what? *Nobody came!* They found out for the first time what it takes to sell a team when no one is buying. No demand existed because they had made no connection in the local community. No one went out and established relationships or communicated with the local businesspeople and politicians. Worst of all, no one really knew how to sell!

The good news is they quickly realized their mistake. However, there is a shortage of good professional sports and marketing executives who have been successful selling tickets to help fill this need. The NBDL realized that their two main revenue streams would be from ticket sales and sponsorship sales and while they did have NBA money coming in, they did not have any television revenue of their own. Therefore, ticket sales were essential and creating a front office dedicated to selling tickets became their primary focus. They now need people who know how to sell tickets in the local community—people like you entering the exciting professional career of ticket sales!

The decline of attendance in professional sports simply means one thing. Teams will need to continue recruiting, training, and hiring more sales professionals; those who can build long-term relationships and bring in ticket sales revenue dollars via direct selling methods. If teams could simply place ads and draw the fans they need, they would, but time is proving that they need to do more than advertise their games. This creates an opportunity for you. *Remember, sports ticket sales are declining; they need you!*

CHAPTER 3

Lucky Beginnings in Sales

I had a lucky beginning to my professional ticket sales career even though it did not start in professional sports. I began my career as an insurance sales representative which, in retrospect, is what I attribute most to my overall success in ticket sales.

Once I was out of college I knew that I needed to make money and start reaping the rewards of my four-year degree. Plus my parents, who were supporting me in the interim, were getting antsy and expected me to be out on my own. I thought that if I had to work, it might as well be an industry that I loved such as sports or music. It has always been my belief that if you truly love what you are doing for a living, work is more of a hobby than a job. After realizing I had no musical talent (which threw that idea out the window), I decided to pursue a career in professional sports.

After researching the industry, I realized three things:

1. There were not many published jobs in sports. I did not see sports positions advertised in the classifieds section of newspapers.
2. I would most likely have to relocate from my hometown in upstate New York if I wanted a job in sports. I grew up in a minor league sports town and other sports companies did not have offices in my town.
3. There appeared to be a lack of entry-level positions in sports. I sent resumes to every professional team that I had an interest in with no results. Like most people in search of sports jobs, I sent cover letters inquiring

about positions in marketing, community relations, or public relations. I did not send out one resume looking for a job in sales.

Sending out resume after resume only led to rejection letter after rejection letter; all of which were form letters indicating that there were no entry-level positions available and that my resume would be kept on file.

Consequently, I became frustrated with the process and interviewed for and accepted a position with a Berkshire life insurance firm in Buffalo, New York. This company offered a great base salary, benefits, and a career start in what was supposed to a "marketing" position. I was hired as a marketing apprentice, helping to market products such as life insurance, disability insurance, and 401(k) plans to the corporate community.

What I did not realize at the time was that they began training me as a sales professional. I was taught all aspects of the sales cycle including how to prospect for new business, conduct fact-finding needs-analysis meetings, give sales presentations, follow up after meetings, close the sale, and service the sold account.

Not knowing anything about sales when I started, I quickly realized that in the insurance industry, if they did not go out and get customers, they would be out of business. I remember asking questions such as, "How do you handle incoming calls or leads from customers who call the agency?" or "When people come into the office looking for insurance, how do you decide which sales representative handles the account?" I somehow envisioned working for this company would be like working in a tennis pro shop where people simply come in to the store looking to buy tennis racquets. What I didn't realize was that there were *no* incoming calls, *no* people walking into the office to buy, and *no* companies calling to inquire about 401(k) plans.

No one seemed interested in this company or even knew that it existed for that matter. I distinctly remember thinking to myself, "If no one ever came into this office, how in world did they get business?"

They did so by going out and *getting* every customer. In reality, it was an *extremely* successful business, because they had professional sales people representing their company and bringing in sales. Here is where I truly began to learn about all the aspects of the sales process including:

1. **Prospecting.** Before you can do anything in sales, you have to learn how to find and identify your prospects. Who will you call on and why will you call them? I learned many research techniques on how to find targeted prospects who had a higher propensity to do business with us.

2. **Cold Calling.** The dreaded term you've probably heard before, cold calling! I had to call companies, homeowners, and individuals—all people that knew nothing about our company—and try to set up meetings.

3. **Fact Finding.** Many people call this doing a "needs analysis" where you learn the needs of your prospect. They had excellent techniques for executing "fact finding" with all of their prospects. You could not present a product to someone until you conducted this fact-finding session to learn the needs of all prospective clients.

4. **Presenting.** Conducting a sales presentation is one of the most important parts of the sales process. I was taught how to conduct a proper sales presentation. We always prepared a solid sales presentation based on what we learned about a prospect's needs during the fact-finding session.

5. **Following Up.** I learned how to diligently follow up with a prospect and get them to make a decision. Many prospects would not make a decision based on the first sales presentation. We were taught how to be skilled at following up to get a sale.

6. **Closing.** The most important part of the sales process is going for the close! We learned many closing techniques to convince a prospect to become a client of our firm.

7. **Servicing.** Once the sale is made, the relationship with the customer begins. Providing a high level of customer service is extremely important in order to keep clients over the long term.

At the time I had no idea that I was leaning how to implement all parts of the sales process, which ultimately lead to my success in sports sales. The problem with my particular job at the life insurance company was that I simply wasn't passionate about insurance products. Selling 401(k) programs, disability insurance, and annuities just didn't fire me up every day.

Furthermore, the deeper I got into selling insurance, the more they wanted me sell to family members to generate quick revenue, something that made me uncomfortable. In the end, I realized that I couldn't do a good job selling insurance because I lacked a passion for the product.

There is no doubt that starting off in life insurance sales was a blessing in disguise. Some of the most successful people I know in ticket sales have benefited from gaining sales experience outside of professional sports. Copier, radio, telemarketing, and insurance sales are all excellent industries in which to get started in sales. They provide training to teach entry-level candidates the basic sales tools necessary to be successful. When you take the tools you have learned in other industries and apply these techniques to professional sports sales, it becomes much easier.

There is one story from my insurance sales days that I would like to share before ending this chapter. When I was selling insurance, I needed to have ten to fifteen sales meetings scheduled each week. This is a great expectation for any sales rep, because if you can deliver this type of sales activity, you will have success.

If I didn't have at least ten meetings scheduled for the following business week by the end of day Friday, I had to stay late and make cold calls to try and boost the level of appointments I had for the following week.

I hated this expectation and had no idea why they wanted me to have this many meetings. I panicked every week, because

I knew that if I didn't have enough meetings booked, I would have to stay late and make calls. Because I was new at the business and had few contacts, this was a common occurrence.

What made matters worse was that there was a pub across the street that the entire office went to every Friday night for happy hour. On Fridays, this pub would serve $5 pitchers of beer and 10-cent buffalo wings (the best in Buffalo!).

There I was a twenty-two-year-old kid right out of school sitting in my dingy office (with no windows), pounding out cold calls with my manager sitting in the room. Meanwhile, everyone else was across the street at happy hour. At any age, this is a pretty bad thing, but at age twenty-two, this was probably the worst thing that could happen. My manager, of course, also wanted to go to happy hour, so he would push me hard and coached me after every call to help get more appointments scheduled.

I remember hating this more than anything, hearing everyone leave the office laughing and joking, knowing I had at least an hour or two of cold calls ahead of me before my first pint. Talk about motivation to book sales meetings!

In conclusion, I was fortunate to get my professional sales career start selling in an industry other than professional sports. What I learned during my first six months in professional insurance sales was the main reason why I believe I've had success in selling tickets.

The good sales habits that I learned, when applied to sports ticket sales, equaled success. People actually returned my calls, were excited to learn more about my product, and occasionally would call into our office. All the things that almost never happened selling insurance did happen selling professional sports tickets. However, because I never expected these things to happen, I never relied on them and always made sure my sales activity was high.

Those that gain sales experience outside of sports will certainly have an edge over other candidates who do not. Also, working for a sales director who has a sales background is a plus. More ticket sales directors are coming from outside of sports and in my experience they are the most successful.

However, there are still a lot of sales directors who come from the sports industry and in my opinion, they are at a disadvantage. Although ticket sales is a challenging profession, it is not nearly as challenging as selling in other industries. Finally, I was also fortunate to start my professional ticket sales career working for a minor league baseball team. Selling minor league baseball tickets is tough and minor league baseball must be as creative as any sports franchise trying to figure out ways to sell tickets. They are also great at developing promotions to help drive ticket sales. Combining my insurance sales background with a minor league baseball background has helped me lead a successful sports selling career.

You, too, can have a successful sport career starting off in ticket sales. If you do little things right every day and have passion for the sport you are selling, you will have success.

CHAPTER 4

Ticket Sales Misconceptions

Many misconceptions exist about ticket sales and the profession of sales in general. The first thing that comes to mind when most people hear the word "salesperson" is the image of the "sleazy" used car salesperson who tries to pressure you into a buying a car you are not sure you want. Or perhaps you think of the audio equipment salesperson who tries to sell you a high-priced piece of stereo equipment with an extended warranty that you really don't need. Or worse yet, you think of that annoying telemarketer who bothers you at home during dinner.

Although there are reasons why these stereotypes exist, most are due to a complete lack of understanding of what sales is really all about. Here are some common misconceptions that exist about ticket sales:

1. All ticket salespeople are sleazy high-pressure salespeople, just like in other industries.
2. All ticket salespeople are telemarketers who cold-call people at home during dinner.
3. Ticket sales is only an entry-level position, a way to get your "foot in the door," so you can ultimately work in other departments.
4. Ticket sales is not as glamorous as marketing, public relations, or community relations.
5. Ticket sales is grueling hard work in which you get rejected all the time.
6. No one wants to talk to ticket salespeople.

7. Ticket salespeople only care about commissions and making the sale.
8. No one really wants to be in ticket sales.
9. No one respects ticket salespeople.
10. Ticket sales is the worst position in a sports team.

Following is the reality of ticket sales based on my experiences, which perhaps will dispel some of the stereotypes and myths surrounding the profession of sales.

1. All ticket sales people are sleazy, high-pressure salespeople.

Although this perception may be true about some ticket salespeople, generally speaking "sleazy" ticket sales tactics will only work in the short term. You may get sales by pressuring prospects into buying tickets from you, but it can jeopardize future long-term relationships.

"Sleazy" sales tactics employ high-pressure techniques to slam prospects into buying. This often means over promising in order to get a sale, then falling short of expectations by not delivering on what was promised. Individuals looking to build strong business relationships for the long term will not be successful with this tactic. Shortsighted, slam-dunk, high-pressure sales tactics might work for some in the short term, but simply will not work over time.

You do, however, have to be aggressive and persistent in order to get a sale, but this can be done with the customer's best interests in mind while limiting the number of promises made to the customer in order to get the sale. You also should sell by suggesting the right product for the customer at the right time. The best ticket salespeople learn their prospect's needs, then suggest the right product to meet those needs. Having professionalism, integrity, and the ability to build trust is critical to future ticket sales success.

2. All ticket salespeople are telemarketers who cold call people at home during dinner.

It is true that ticket sales sometimes requires calling people at their homes after work hours, telemarketing to various lists. However, most sports teams now use closely targeted lists when making these calls. Most individuals who ticket sales reps call on are usually from lists of people who have been to games, purchased tickets, or signed up for fan clubs or e-mail lists.

Thus, the lists are more qualified and the initial calls are usually fact finding rather than cold sales calls. When using targeted lists, people actually want to talk to the caller because they have been to a game and might be fans of the team. Other companies' telemarketing efforts appear to be random shotgun-type approach. I am always amazed at the number of calls I receive from telemarketers asking me to buy something when I am not in any way a qualified prospect for them.

Just the other day I received a telemarketing call trying to sell me opera tickets. As someone who has never attended an opera nor has any intention of ever doing so, I cannot understand how my name ended up on their list or which list they were using for that matter. Obviously they are using "untargeted" lists. Furthermore, the National Do-Not-Call list registry will impact untargeted telemarketing practices. This law will force companies to build more targeted databases and find more qualified prospects to call on who have expressed some interest in their product. Sports teams will also have to be smarter about how they build and acquire their lists and be aware of the Do-Not-Call registry. Time will tell how this impacts professional sports teams, however, if teams are smart, they will not be all that affected by this law.

So while you will probably have to make calls to people's homes when you start off selling tickets, they are usually to people who have some affiliation to your sport or have expressed some interest in your team. Additionally, most sales professionals recognize and appreciate people's dinner schedules and will often refrain from calling during dinner hours.

3. Ticket sales is only an entry-level position, a way to get your "foot in the door" so you can ultimately work in other departments.

Ticket sales does indeed provide the best entry-level opportunity available in professional sports. However, ticket sales is not only an entry-level position. Many ticket sales reps experience a great deal of success and remain in sales for the duration of their sports career. Also, many successful ticket sales reps have had previous sales experience in another industry.

Therefore, if you have been successful selling tickets for another sports team or if you have had nonsports sales experience, you become an attractive sales candidate to sports teams. Some teams may pay a higher base salary for candidates with sales experience, plus others are willing to grant existing accounts to experienced reps joining their organization. This, of course, makes getting started with a new team easier because by inheriting accounts, you don't have to build your book of business from scratch.

The natural progression of a successful sales representative would be to graduate into sales management. However, a lucrative career as a sales representative for many years is possible.

I used to think that if I started off in sales, I could move to other, more glamorous positions. The truth of the matter is, no matter how far my career advances, I will always want to be part of the revenue-generating side of the business.

I believe sales is the most rewarding part of the professional sports business. If more people took a sales approach to their jobs in other positions, I believe they would be more successful. Most good things happen in business if you take a proactive approach to your business, whereas, if you sit back and wait for things to happen, most of the time nothing will.

Ticket sales is certainly a great way to get your foot in the door and it will also put you in a position to look at other opportunities in the team's front office. If you are successful in ticket sales, teams will indeed find a way to keep you as part of their staff.

You can have a very rewarding career in sales and you may find, like me, that once you get a taste of sales success, the other career opportunities all of a sudden don't appear as attractive as they once might have.

4. Sales is not as glamorous as marketing, public relations, or community relations.

Some people might argue this is true. I actually used to feel the same way about this statement, however, the more I learned about ticket sales and realized that I loved it, the less appealing those other positions became. To me, there is nothing better than experiencing sales success and growing business for your team.

Adding a new corporate relationship to the team or closing a large group sale that you know would have never occurred if it were not for your proactive sales efforts makes this profession extremely rewarding.

I lose respect for people who think they are "too good" for sales. It takes a certain amount of courage to be able to pick up the phone, face rejection, and call someone to try and develop a sales relationship. Many people simply cannot do it. Therefore, it is easier to look down on sales because most people know deep down that they cannot sell if they had to do it themselves.

In my opinion, marketing, public relations, or community relations are not as glamorous as ticket sales. Plus, all of those positions would not exist if the salespeople representing their teams do not have success selling tickets. So everyone in a sports organization should be grateful for the job that ticket sales professionals do!

Developing business relationships, bringing in revenue dollars, and seeing the stands filled are rewarding to me. I also like being on the front lines of the decision-making process for our business. Because generating revenue is the most important aspect of every sports team, as the vice president of ticket sales, I am part of many key business decisions.

The same cannot be said with people in other positions. Positions such as PR and team administration are simply the administrators of policy and oftentimes not policy makers.

5. Ticket Sales is grueling, hard work where you get rejected all the time.

Ticket sales is hard work where you do get rejected a good percentage of the time. However, you do not get rejected all the time, and when you do, it is not you they are rejecting but your product and/or your team.

At times ticket sales can be very grueling and there are many aspects of the job that are demanding. Cold calling, for example, can be difficult, but the more you do it, the better you get. The better you get at sales, the less you have to rely on cold calling because you become better at prospecting and asking for referrals.

Attending three or four meetings a day and going to networking events after hours can also be taxing, but it is all part of the job and the more grueling you make a sales job, the more success you will have. The great thing about ticket sales is that the harder you work, the more you will sell. Ultimately you will reap the rewards of your hard work and efforts. There is no other position that has the direct pay off in results for hard work than in ticket sales.

6. No one wants to talk to ticket salespeople.

At times this might seem to be a true statement, especially when you are first starting off in ticket sales. However, the reason it appears no one wants to speak with you is that people are often simply too busy to talk to ticket salespeople. There might be times when no one will call you back. Actually you should never expect prospects to call you back. It may or may not be that they don't want to talk with you, but it certainly means that you rank near the bottom of their priority list on who to call back.

Unfortunately, I am as guilty as the next person about not returning calls from salespeople. Some of the time, I actually do want to speak with sales reps offering various products and services that I might need. However, I rarely call them back, because I am so busy and by nature of the game, they are the last people I call back. I often rush a salesperson off the phone or ask them to call me back at a more convenient time. Speaking with a sales rep, interested or not, is low on my priority list. In fact, I feel that it is a sales person's obligation to be persistent and call me back if they really want my business. It is up to them to contact me and hunt me down to speak with me during a convenient time. They must earn their sale.

So, although many people might not want to talk with you at the beginning of the sales contact, if you establish a need and then a good relationship, over time you will find many people that will talk with you and ultimately will enjoy speaking with you. You simply need to stay persistent and keep trying to find prospects that will want to talk with you.

7. Ticket salespeople only care about commissions and making the sale.

Ticket salespeople do not only care about earning commission dollars. However, I would argue that if the extra money earned through commissions by making sales does not motivate you, even just a little bit, than perhaps you shouldn't be looking at a career start in ticket sales.

You will find that while making commission dollars is important to sales professionals, it is usually not the most important thing. Most successful ticket salespeople enjoy "winning" the sale, helping the team succeed, and being recognized as much as they enjoy receiving a commission check at the end of the month.

Bonuses and commissions are simply the tangible payoff method that most teams have in place as incentives to help motivate sales reps to sell more. Commissions are certainly a motivating factor for me and another reason why I like sales. Why not get paid higher dollars for the long hours and hard work that you put in? Plus, if you are delivering for a sports team, why should you not share in the financial rewards.

My experience with all types of sales professionals is that commissions only partially motivate them. Each individual is obviously different, and as a sales manager, you must find the things that motivate each rep within your department. However, commissions usually rank behind some of the things I just mentioned. Most reps simply enjoy being around the professional game, love the team and want to succeed, and then be recognized for their accomplishments.

8. No one really wants to be in ticket sales.

Most people simply do not know they want to be in sales because no one told them about the upside of being in ticket sales. I would argue that people who think they don't want to be in sales never took the time to learn more about it.

I hope that by reading this book, a lot more people will want to go into ticket sales and that other people within the sports industry will look at ticket sales from a different perspective. If you want to break into sports and succeed, then you too should consider ticket sales!

9. No one respects ticket salespeople.

This statement is also simply not true, especially if you are a true sales professional. As in most industries, if you are unprofessional, no one will respect you no matter what department you are working in. Although some people may not respect ticket salespeople to begin with, you can quickly prove them wrong.

If people won't respect you right away, make them respect you by rising above this perception. Those who don't respect ticket salespeople are usually ignorant to what it takes to be successful in sales. Once you gain someone's respect, you will never lose it if you continue to do the things that gained their respect in the first place.

The toughest job that I've had to do in ticket sales is to build respect and credibility of the ticket sales department. Like everything else, a certain level of respect is always due to people in any position. However, the remainder of the respect has to be earned.

You earn respect by having success, acting professional, and having integrity in the way you conduct yourself. In the end, having a high level of sales success will earn everyone's respect.

10. Ticket sales is the worst position in a sports team.

This unfortunately is the perception of some people working in a sports organization. However, it is often due to people's own fears about ticket sales. The reality is, without ticket sales, many sports teams simply would not survive. All jobs within a sports organization depend on a successful ticket sales effort.

I feel that ticket sales is the *best* position that you could be in working for a professional sports team. Especially when you are new and starting off in the business, there is *no* better position for you to be in than the ticket sales department. No matter what your future aspirations are within a sports team, having a ticket sales background will help you succeed in any position within the front office of a sports team.

In the end, it's really up to you to decide this on your own. I love ticket sales and think it is an amazing profession, however, ticket sales can difficult if you are not the right person for the job or if you are unwilling to do the little things daily in order to succeed.

Ticket sales has many rewards that far outweigh the challenges. I simply think most people who don't like sales are basing this on perception and not reality. I think many people are afraid of selling. They are afraid of the rejection they would face and the fact that they are leaving themselves vulnerable to their fears. Most people choose to avoid areas of discomfort and that is why they would rather not be in sales.

In my opinion these people are simply misinformed and perhaps a bit ignorant to what ticket sales are truly about. People could learn a lot about themselves if they overcome the fear of rejection, picked up the phone, and made a cold call. It's not as bad as one might think. By overcoming objections and the fear of rejection, you become a stronger person.

In summary, there are many misconceptions about the ticket sales profession. Almost all of these misconceptions and negative perceptions are made by people who do not truly understand what ticket sales is all about. If you focus on all of the negative aspects of ticket sales, then one would conclude that this profession would be the worst in the sports business.

However, if you look at what really happens day to day in ticket sales, then you will change your perception. Success breeds more success and the more success you have, the more fun you will have selling tickets. You need to focus on the positives of being in ticket sales and I assure you they will out weigh the negatives. Ticket sales is your key to success in the professionals sports world.

CHAPTER 5

Characteristics of Successful Ticket Sales Professionals

In order to be successful in sales, there are certain characteristics that you should possess. Many candidates trying to land jobs in professional sports have character traits that will allow them to be successful in sales. However, most don't know they possess them, much less what they are.

Qualities of a Good Salesperson

You may have seen some of the following characteristics mentioned as prerequisites for sales jobs. You should look closely at these to see if they match yours. If you don't possess the majority of these qualities, it doesn't necessarily mean that you won't succeed in sales. It simply means that you'll have to work harder to compensate for lacking characteristics that equal sales success. If you possess many or all of them, then you have a better chance at being successful in ticket sales.

Furthermore, the traits that you possess from this list are your sales strengths and should be your focus when starting out in sales. You should identify your weaknesses and do your best to improve on them. The following is a listing of some of the traits I believe you must possess to be successful in sales.

1. **You believe in the sport and the product you are selling.**

If you don't love the sport you are selling and truly believe that fans should go to watch the games, you will have a challenging time selling tickets. Like in any sales position, you have to believe in your product.

A passion for your product is a key for success. It is difficult to sell a product you don't believe in. If you feel you would not buy your product yourself, then you will have a difficult time convincing others to buy.

2. You consider yourself to be a "people person."

If you are an outgoing person and enjoy being around people, you have another basic personality trait to be successful in ticket sales. Interacting and being around people is another key to success.

Part of being successful in ticket sales is being able to interact well with others. If you enjoy being in social settings and environments and meeting as many people as possible, then you have positive personality trait for sales. It would be difficult for someone who considers him or herself an introvert to be successful in sales.

3. You are a team player.

Most successful salespeople are also true team players. Having individual success in sales is critical; however, the most successful ticket sales departments work well as a team. A sales staff built of team players makes for a more professional environment in which to achieve success. If you are someone who enjoys personal success while also being part of a team, you have yet another positive personality trait to help you be successful in sales.

4. You are competitive in nature and "want to win."

People who are competitive in nature make excellent sale professionals. In the sales position postings listed in the classified ads, you will see employers seeking people who are competitive. That is because in sales you must compete to win all the time.

Every day you are competing to win in sales, competing against other teams in your market as well competing against other sales representatives in your own organization. Often competitive athletes have great success in selling tickets. Those who have held leadership positions such as club presidents or team captains for their respective high school or college sports teams are always high on my list of sales candidates.

5. You have confidence in yourself and your abilities.

Having confidence in yourself as well as in your abilities is a critical trait of successful ticket salespeople. Having high self-esteem also goes hand in hand with this personality trait. If you don't have confidence in yourself and believe in what you are doing, you'll have a challenging time dealing with the rejection that often comes with sales.

Sales is a tough profession where you will be tested throughout your career. You must always remain confident in yourself and what your abilities can bring to the table. You must always carry yourself with a high level of self-esteem in order to face a lot of the day-to-day rejection that you will encounter.

6. You are a self-starter and a self-motivator.

Some front-office teams have compensation and incentive plans that are very rewarding and motivating. Good sales managers will find ways to create motivation within the sales office, but no matter how good or weak the sales system or management is, in the end, motivation must come from within.

Many sales teams may not have great sales plans, incentives, or rewards to help keep you motivated. But even if you have solid motivational tools and incentives coming from the office environment in which you are in, you still must be able to motivate yourself to do the necessary things day in and day out that will lead you to be successful.

If you can motivate yourself, regardless of the environment around you, you have yet another characteristic to be successful in ticket sales.

Unfortunately, I have been in some pretty unmotivating and uninspiring sales environments. There were many situations where I simply could have passed blame for a lot of reasons as to why I could not be successful. However, I have always been self-motivated to do as well as I possibly could in order to succeed despite circumstances that have been around me.

7. You are dedicated to your profession.

If you are the type of person who can stay dedicated to your job and say, "I will do whatever it takes to be successful," then you have yet another positive trait for a ticket sales position.

Being successful in sales takes commitment and dedication to being the best that you can be. Like with any profession, you should also be dedicated to learning as much as you can about sales. Reading this book is a great start, but you must continue to learn about the profession of sales, attending sales seminars, reading books and listening to sales audio tapes to continue your sales development and get the job done.

8. You plan for success and can set goals.

You may have heard the old saying in business, "Most people don't plan to fail, they fail to plan." The most successful sales professionals develop a solid sales plan. If you are someone who can develop a personal plan, then you have another trait that will lead you to sales success.

You must also be able to set goals. Developing a plan and being able to set goals are keys to ticket sales success. If you have set goals in your life until now and have been successful in achieving them, you have yet another quality that will help you lead a successful sales career. We will focus on goal setting in Chapter 7, because it is critical to sales success.

9. You must be able to face rejection and deal with objections.

The best ticket professionals face and effectively deal with rejection on a daily basis. Keep in mind that the best sales professionals can close 30 to 35 percent of their business prospects. This means that 70 percent of your prospects will not buy from you. More people won't buy from you than will, so if you can put this rejection in perspective and deal with facing this daily, you have yet another positive sales characteristic.

10. You must be able maintain your composure and professionalism when facing adversity.

As with any sales, ticket sales come with a lot of highs and lows. You must be able to not get too frustrated when things go bad and must be able to deal with difficult situations. You must be able to keep a happy medium in the roller coaster world of sales.

There will be months when things are going extremely well, but then there will be months when things are going horribly bad. You must be able to keep a level head in order to deal with the highs and the lows. If you can maintain your composure, especially when times are tough in sales, you will have an easier time as a sales professional than those who cannot deal with adversity.

Identify Your Sales Traits

If you find that you possess many of these characteristics, the news is good for you. You should strongly consider ticket sales as a starting point for your sports career. I feel that I have many of these personality traits and that they have helped me to lead a successful ticket sales career.

If someone had pointed out to me early in my career that ticket sales fit my personality traits, I would have looked for ways to learn more about this as profession. Therefore, if you have read this chapter on personality traits and find yourself nodding your head "yes" to many, if not all, you are on the right track starting off in ticket sales.

.

CHAPTER 6

How to Get the Interview and Land the Job

How to Get the Interview

Once you decide that ticket sales is the career path for you, then it is time to get the all-important interview. Because you will be trying to land a job in sales, you should take a proactive sales approach to getting the interview. You simply cannot send out a pile of resumes and hope for the best. You have to take matters into your own hands and convince sales directors that they should interview you.

Following are three critical steps to help you land that important interview. Amazingly enough, as simple as these steps sound, few, if any, candidates follow them.

Step 1: Decide you want to be in ticket sales and *say it on your resume.*

If you have decided that you want to get your career path started in sales, you are already ahead of the competition. If this is the case, then you should state it on your resume. Believe me when I tell you that I receive few, if any, resumes or cover letters that state their position objective is to land a "position in ticket sales."

Having this clearly stated on your resume and cover letter will give you a huge advantage in securing an interview, as it will automatically differentiate your resume from the piles of other resumes seeking a "Position in marketing" or "Position in community relations" or "Position in public relations." Reading this on a resume will be seen as a breath of fresh air for most sales directors.

Along with stating you want a job in ticket sales on your resume and cover letter, you should also include reference to your sales-related experiences from internships, classes, or activities. It could include retail sales experience or something as simple as helping a charitable organization raise funds. If you have any telemarketing experience, that is a huge bonus, so be sure to highlight this on your resume as well.

Step 2: Call the director of sales.

Now that you have sent in your resume stating that you want a job in ticket sales, remember you still simply cannot leave it to chance that you will get an interview. You are trying to get a position in ticket sales so you need to take the next proactive step and that is calling the director of sales (DOS). Even if a job posting states, "No phone calls please," it doesn't matter. You should still call.

Typically I include this language in my job listings to limit the number of calls, but I *always* take calls from interested candidates who say they want a job in ticket sales. I want to see who is aggressive enough to make a phone call and am impressed by candidates who call me trying to set up an interview. This is a similar exercise to calling a decision-maker to schedule a sales meeting, a talent they will need to have in order to succeed in ticket sales.

If you get the DOS on the phone, tell them how excited you are that you got in touch with him or her and that you would like to interview for a *ticket sales position.* Of the phone calls I receive, I get very few, if any, people calling to ask me specifically about positions in ticket sales. For some reason, it appears that most candidates confuse me with the human resources director, because they usually call me looking for "any openings that might exist" within our organization.

You should inquire about current opportunities that exist in ticket sales, and then request an interview. This in and of itself will differentiate you even further from other candidates.

Even if a job is not currently open, you should still ask for an interview. There is usually turnover in many ticket sales departments. Sales is a tough profession and it is not for everyone. Sometimes the wrong people get into ticket sales for the wrong reasons. Many people go into ticket sales not knowing what it takes to be successful. This often results in turnover within sales departments.

Therefore, even if a job is not open today, there is a good chance a position might open up in the future. Most DOSs will agree to an informational interview about ticket sales where you can learn more about what they are looking for and at the same time, they can learn more about you as a sales candidate.

It would be very rare for a DOS not agree to an informational-type interview regarding a sales position. They might, however, be hesitant to grant an informational-type interview from a candidate who is interested (just like everyone else) in a position in CR, PR, or marketing

Step 3: Be persistent and follow up on your call.

If you do not get the interview during the first call to the DOS, leave a voice mail message and then call again. I suggest you stay persistent until you at least have a conversation with the DOS so you can introduce yourself. This will immediately differentiate you from other candidates.

Just like in sales where you need to follow up with prospects, it is important to follow up with the DOS. If you left a voice mail message and did not receive a call back, simply call back a few days later. Stay persistent. It will pay off in the end.

You can also send an e-mail to the DOS with your resume and cover letter attached. Having the e-mail address of the DOS can also be helpful in the follow up process, whether you send a follow-up e-mail to confirm an interview, confirm a follow-up phone call date, or simply send a follow-up thank you note.

You should be able to find the DOS's e-mail address on the team's Web site or media guide. You can also call anyone in the team's front office and ask him or her if they can give you the e-mail address for the director of sales. It shouldn't take that much digging to find out what their e-mail address is.

In summary, you should approach getting an interview just like you would approach any new business prospect. In order to give yourself the best chance of landing a job, you must take the correct proactive steps in order to land an interview. If you follow the three simple steps I just described, you will land an interview for a ticket sales position. Follow them, get the interview and begin your career in professional ticket sales.

How to Land the Job

Now that you've landed the all-important interview, it's time to land the job! This is your time to shine. My best advice for how to approach an interview would be to treat the interview as a sales call. During a sales call, you must convince the prospect that they should buy from you, thus you should treat a ticket sales interview in the same manner. "Sell" the DOS on the concept that you are the right person for the job. However, before you go to the interview, you must first *prepare!*

Step 1: Research

It is crucial that you do some basic research prior to the interview to learn facts about the team with which you are interviewing. Research the team, the league, and the executives who will be interviewing you. This will immediately raise your level of credibility and help differentiate you from other candidates. Nothing frustrates an interviewer more than interviewing candidates who are unprepared. I can often tell within the first five to ten minutes whether or not a candidate has done their homework.

Too many candidates come into an interview completely unprepared. A job interview could be a one-chance opportunity to land the job for which you are looking. Why would you leave it to chance and "wing" the sales interview? You should prepare and do your homework. You always feel better taking a test that you have prepared for versus taking a test that you didn't, so why would you approach an interview without the same amount of preparation?

It is expected that you at least have a basic knowledge of the team and league for which you will be selling. Familiarize yourself with simple facts such as the team's record, how long the team has been around, last post season appearance, and so forth.

It is also a good idea to learn a little bit about the person who will be interviewing you as well as any other executives in the office with whom you may meet. If you learn an interesting fact about the person interviewing you and reference it during the interview, you will automatically increase your opportunity to land an offer—especially if the person with whom you are interviewing was recently promoted, won an award, or was recognized within his or her profession. Mentioning this will make a good impression on the interviewer, because it is human nature to like hearing good things said about you.

You should also learn the names of the key people in the organization such as the owner, general manager, team president, and head coach as well as a handful of star players. This is important information that most people will assume you already know.

Finally, you should familiarize yourself with business facts such as ticket prices, ticket plans, and general ticket promotions. The more educated you are, the more qualified you will appear during an interview. Plus, knowing the team and organization will also give you confidence heading into the interview

The best place to gather information about a team is through the team's Web site, as all professional teams and leagues have one. Official team Web sites are a great tool because they contain most of the information for which you are looking. As a side note, you can also learn some interesting facts by going on "un-official" team Web sites and fan pages as it can help you learn some unique things about the team from a fan's perspective. Sometimes rumors and general fan gossip will give you a better understanding about some of the issues teams are dealing with. Collectively, all of this information will help you better prepare for the interview.

Another great source for information is the team's media guide. All professional teams produce an official team media guide for distribution to the press. Media guides contain all the information you ever needed to know from front office staff to players to stadium and ticket information.

You can usually purchase a media guide on the team's Web site or simply call the PR office and request one. Most team PR offices will usually send out a complimentary media guide, especially if you tell them you need it for a research paper or something like that.

Finally, because you will be interviewing for a ticket sales position, you should learn as much as you can about the team's ticket plans, groups sales, and pricing. You can call any team's sales department and request ticket information and they will send it to you. You might even strike up a conversation with an existing sales rep that you can use to learn more information about a team.

Taking a few extra minutes to prepare for an interview by doing research on the team will automatically put you ahead of other candidates interviewing for the same job. In addition, knowing the team and its organization will give you greater confidence heading into the interview.

Step 2: Prepare Educated Questions

Now that you've learned all you can about the organization, it is time for you to prepare quality questions to ask during the interview. Most interviewers should and will give candidates the opportunity to ask questions. In turn, you should be prepared to ask solid educated questions.

What is discussed during the interview will determine the questions that you most likely will want to ask. However, you should be ready to go with good questions. Do not lead off your questions by asking about salary, benefits, vacation, or bonuses. Of course, any job candidate will want to know that information. However, those types of questions should be saved for the very end of the interview process rather than the beginning. During a job interview you want to learn about all of the aspects of the job and the office you will be working in. The interviewer will want to know if you will be someone who will succeed in sales as well as someone who will fit into the office culture. Therefore, they are looking for people that are interested in the job and not in how much money they will make.

Here are some topics about which to ask questions concerning the organization and position:

- *Interesting things you learned about the interviewer.* This shows interest in the interviewer.

  "I see you left the Washington Bullets to pursue a career with DC United of the Major League Soccer; why did you make that decision?"
  "I see you got your career start selling insurance. How different is insurance sales from professional sports sales?"

- *Questions about an award or achievement earned by the interviewer.* This shows you appreciate those who achieve at high levels.

  "I see your team lead the league in attendance last season. To what would you attribute your great success in ticket sales?"
  "I see that you won the Team Ticketing Award when you were at DC United. How did your sales team win that award?"

- *Questions about the team or the league* and perhaps some challenges they are facing. This demonstrates you know some about the team and its league.

  "I saw your league's television ratings decreased slightly last season. What factors do you think contributed to the decline in ratings?"
  "I see attendance went down slightly last season, to what do you attribute this decline?"

"I see your league is thinking about expanding by two teams next season. Why is the league looking to do this and do you think it will have a positive or negative effect?"

- *Questions about other executives working in the office.* This shows you have researched who the key people are within the organization.

"I've been reading a lot about your general manager who has been quoted in the papers recently. What is it like to work for your GM and what type of front office is he trying to build?"
"I saw that your supervisor had an article in the *Sports Business Journal* about your marketing strategies. Do you feel your strategies are working as well as was stated in the article?"

- *Questions about sales team programs.* This shows you took the time to learn about the team's particular sales programs.

"I read about your Camp Partnership Program. Has that program been successful? It looks like a great program."
"I saw your Kicks for Kids clients listed in the *FREE-KICK Game Day* magazine. What are the details behind the Kicks for Kids program that have led you to have as many corporate clients as you have?"

- *Questions about a success story.* This shows you appreciate success and recognize success.

"I read that your team grew its corporate season ticket base by 118 percent. What factors contributed to this off-the-field success?"
"I saw that your team led the league in group sales. Why did you have such great year selling group tickets?"

- *Questions about advancement opportunities.* These are very important questions because they demonstrate you are the type of person looking for advancement opportunities.

"If I lead the sales team in sales over the next two years, what type of advancement opportunities exist within your team?"

- *Questions about office structure, internal support, training, and general team environment*

    "What type of customer service support does your front-office team have for its ticket sales department?"
    "What type of sales training do you provide?"
    "How would you describe the team environment within your sales team?"

Time for the Interview: Highlight Your Strengths!

In Chapter 5, I discussed the characteristics that you should possess in order to be successful in ticket sales. During the interview, you must demonstrate that you possess these characteristics and in particular, highlight those characteristics that are your strengths.

Learning About the Candidate

For starters, as a team executive, I want to learn about a candidate's background and education and how they relate to sales. I am also looking for previous leadership roles, such as a captain of a sports teams or a club leader. I also want to look at their professional sales experience. Finally, in their previous work positions, I want to learn why they left—was it to pursue an advancement opportunity or did they leave because they were asked to?

After I learn all the relevant background information, I then want to learn more about the way they work and what they would bring to our organization. I am looking for indicators about the following:

1. What type of overall character does this person have and what type of business ethics do they have?
2. What type of work ethic does this person have?

3. Is this person a team player?
4. Is this person motivated and a self-starter?
5. Will this person be afraid of rejection or objections?
6. What are this person's future goals? Are they ambitious and do they want to further their career?
7. Is the person driven to succeed?
8. Is the person a "people person?" Are they someone from whom I would buy?
9. What type of passion for our product does this candidate have?
10. Will this person do what it takes to succeed in sales?

These are the main questions that I have in mind when interviewing job candidates. I am looking to see how many characteristics they possess that will lead them to ultimately be successful in sales. I often ask many open-ended questions seeking to learn as much as I can about the candidate.

Step 3: Sell the Interviewer

During the interview, you should be confident and answer as honestly as you can. If you are convinced that ticket sales is the way for you to go, the more convincing you are that you possess characteristics that will lead you to sales success, the better chance you have to land the job.

After asking educated questions and discussing your background characteristics, it is time for you to sell the interviewer that you are the best candidate for the job. Tell them how excited you are about the position and the team. Also, tell them how much you want this opportunity and if given the chance that you will do anything it takes to succeed. Be confident in yourself and tell them you will not fail because you are determined to succeed. This confidence will shine through and you will be convincing to the interviewer.

I also recommend highlighting a past sales success story if you have one. Equally effective would be any success story where perhaps you overcame obstacles to achieve a desired result.

One final word of warning: I recommend against saying, "Tickets sales doesn't bother me" or "I have no trouble with sales." For some reason I frequently hear this and it really annoys me. This answer makes it sound as if the candidate believes that ticket sales is a nuisance position that they are willing to tolerate for the short term, while setting sights on other opportunities. Simply stated, never say during an interview that ticket sales doesn't bother you. Instead, say you look forward to the challenges ticket sales provides as well as succeeding in delivering sales results for the team.

In summary, taking a few extra minutes to prepare for an interview by doing research on the team will automatically put you ahead of other candidates interviewing for the same job. Plus, knowing the team and organization will also give you greater confidence heading into the interview. Be sure to prepare and ask relevant questions during the interview. And remember, it is always obvious which candidates come prepared versus those who do not.

CHAPTER 7

How to Succeed in Ticket Sales

Numerous books on how to succeed in sales are available, therefore I will not attempt to rewrite a sales book. I will, however, provide you with a list of the top 15 "tips" to help you succeed in ticket sales. These are proven tips that have personally helped me become successful in selling tickets. I will also provide tips to help you think smarter about prospecting for new business. This chapter will be particularly helpful to new sales reps entering the business and I recommend that sales managers encourage new hires to read it as well. Implementing these tips will lead to ticket sales success.

I once asked the general manager of the MetroStars, Nick Sakiewicz, about the best piece of advice he would give any young sales rep on how to succeed in sales. Recognizing it is difficult to sum up how to succeed in sales in one sentence, his response was a good one. He said, "To be successful in ticket sales, *one must be on an endless pursuit of relationships.*" This is an extremely powerful and true sales statement!

Ticket sales, unlike most other types of sales, is a volume business. The goal is to sell as many tickets to as many people as possible. You need the "nickel-and-dime" smaller sales as much as you need the larger volume sales. If you are on an endless pursuit of relationships, you are bound to find all types of business. The following are what I believe to be the top 15 tips to being successful in ticket sales.

   1. *Recognize that ticket sales is a volume business requiring you to be on an endless pursuit of relationships.* If you go into ticket sales with this general concept in mind, you will already be ahead of the game.

There is an old saying about sales, that sales is a numbers game. Thus, the more contacts and prospects you have, the more chances for success. You need to have a high volume of prospects with whom you are developing relationships at all times. If your sales success ratio were 20 percent, for example, 20 percent of 100 prospects would equal 20 new clients. However, 20 percent of 200 prospects would equal 40 new clients.

High sales activity = Sales success

The higher your sales activity, the better your chances are for success. You cannot have your flyers, your business card, and your e-mail address out to enough people. The more people who have your business contact information, the better your chances of success.

2. *There are things you can control and things you cannot.* Things you can control are the number of calls you make, the number of meetings and appointments you go on, the number of follow-up calls you make, the number of e-mails and faxes you send, plus the number of networking events, seminars, and guest-speaking engagements you attend. Things you cannot control include the team's performance, the economy, team awareness, stadium problems, weather, and dead-end prospects.

Make sure you focus on the things you can control and sales results will come. Adapt to the factors you cannot control, but do not focus on these things; outside factors can quickly lead to excuses as to why you cannot succeed. You should never use things you cannot control as obstacles to your success. Remember, when times are tough you can always make one more phone call, go on one more meeting, or attend one more networking event. Take control of the things you can control!

3. *Referrals, referrals, and more referrals!* Referrals are the single most valuable tool for sales success, yet most sales people do not ask for enough referrals. If you get in the habit of asking for referrals right from the beginning, it will become habitual. Asking for referrals is like starting a new exercise program. At first it is difficult, but eventually it gets easier. Then if you miss an exercise session, you feel terrible. It is the same with referrals. Once you get used to asking for them, you will feel awkward not asking for them.

You will read about the importance of referrals in sales books because they are absolutely critical to sales success. The hardest thing about starting off in sales is building your book of business. However, once you gain clients and do right by them, your existing clients will be a great source of referrals.

Using your network of clients to get referrals to other clients will be critical to your success. If you learn how to ask early for referrals early in your career, you will be far ahead of anyone else.

4. *Ask for and get testimonial letters from your clients.* The goal is to get as many success stories on paper as possible and then tell others about it. If you do right by your clients, they will write testimonial letters for you. Receiving testimonial letters on company or organization's letterhead can be a powerful sales tool.

Using testimonial letters will help you prove to others considering doing business with you and your team that they too will have a positive experience dealing with you. You can then say that your goal is to have them write you a testimonial letter the following season. Although you will get some testimonial letter from happy customers, you still have to ask for them in order to build a solid arsenal of testimonial letters.

I have asked many clients to write testimonial letters, especially clients who have been happy with our team. More often than not, they will write the letter for you. Some have been so happy with our team that they have told me to write the letter for them and they would put it on their letterhead and sign it. Now that is trust from your most loyal clients.

> **5.** *Renewal business is critical to long-term sales success.* Although some teams have customer service support for ticket sales, at the end of the day, your clients are still *your* customers and *you* must provide the best possible customer service. Remember, it is easier to maintain an existing customer than to find a new one.

If an account purchased $1,000 worth of tickets from you in Year 1 and then left after the first year, they would end up being only a $1,000 account to you. However, if they spend $1,000 in Year 1 and $1,000 for the next five years, they now become a $5,000 account for you. *Renewal and repeat business is critical to long-term sales success.*

> **6.** *Mix it up.* Don't put all your eggs in one basket. Do not try only one type of sales approach or one type of sales pitch. You need to experiment with various sales approaches and techniques and test as many different sales methods as possible. You should look to find success stories and identify your strengths and weakness. You must then build on your strengths and try to improve on your weaknesses. Most successful sales people find a sales formula that works and stick with it, but also find a way to adapt their sales methods.

Experiment with calling first, followed up by sending out mail. Then send a fax to your prospects first, then call them. Or you can send information out in the mail, and make a follow-up call or send a personalized e-mail, and make a follow-up call.

Being in sales for a professional team allows you to be very creative in trying to gain a prospect's attention. Most teams will give you some access to team merchandise, complimentary tickets for games, or invitations to private team events. All of these things will make it easier for you to get your foot in the door with a prospect. How many people would not like receiving a free t-shirt in the mail, or a free invite to a sporting event or a complimentary invitation to attend a team luncheon or dinner? Most teams have a ton of events that you can invite prospects to. I even heard one sports sales story where the sales rep sent one autographed basketball sneaker in the mail to a prospect, and told the prospect he'd have to take a meeting with him to get the second one.

Hopefully you get the point. Know your success ratio and mix it up—you will find the approach that is the most successful for you. Another tip: **Do not** send spam e-mails; they are ineffective. Instead, send personalized e-mails when at all possible; they are much more effective.

7. *Stay organized because ticket sales is a unique industry where you actually create work for yourself over time.* Think about it. If you make thirty prospect calls and fifteen of them want you to send information and another ten ask you to call them back, you now have twenty-five next action steps that you must complete.

You must now put together ticket information to send out, mark your calendar for a follow-up calls, and return calls to those requesting a follow-up call immediately. Also, if you attend a business-to-business networking night and meet five people, you now have five more follow-up calls you must make the following day. Over time you can see how contacts and your workload begin to pile up.

Keep good notes. It is important to keep good notes on your calls. The more you can learn about prospects, the better. Make sure you also stay organized for your follow-up calls. If you tell a prospect you will send them something and then call them back the following Tuesday, make sure you send them the information and call them back on that Tuesday!

This is why staying organized is extremely important. You want to make sure you follow up with potential clients when you say you'll follow up and you also don't want to let any prospects fall between the cracks or get lost in the shuffle. This can happen if you don't stay organized. Good sales systems will have computer programs to help you stay organized; these include Act! by Best Software or GoldMine by Front Range. You should find out what type of sales tools the organization has during the interview, but in the end it is up to you to stay organized.

8. *The very best sales professionals maximize what is called "prime time selling."* Prime time selling are the hours when you should be focused on sales activity such as cold calling, making follow-up calls, going on meetings, and setting new meetings. Prime time selling is usually early in the morning, during the heart of the day (aside from the lunch hour), and perhaps early in the evening.

Tasks such as expense reports, putting together proposals and other "maintenance"-type office work should be done during nonprime time selling hours. The best sales professionals treat prime time selling hours like gold and do not let anyone interfere with these precious hours when sales activities should get done.

9. *Don't quit; stay persistent and stay consistent.* There is a saying in the sales industry: "Avoid getting high with the highs or low with the lows." Sales is a cyclical game where there will be peaks and valleys, highs and lows. If you can identify and accept this early in the sales game, you will be all the better in the long run.

Don't get overly excited when you make a big sale, have a big month, or go on a great meeting. Likewise, don't get too low when you go into a sales slump. Keep everything in perspective and realize that there will be good times and bad times. Simply remember that if you stay true to the sales process, you will come out ahead in the long run. Small periods of struggles should not get you so down that you quit.

10. *Keep the pipeline full and don't bank on "that one big sale."* Always keep pushing to develop new business. I have seen too many sales reps fall into the trap of banking on the one big sale. They go to a great meeting where all things seem positive for a huge sale and as a result stop prospecting for new business. The pipeline becomes anything but full. It is easy to let a false sense of security creep in, thinking, "I've got this one big sale coming in this month so I am all set."

When the sale doesn't come in or doesn't happen for a million reasons, the reps are crushed and their month is now ruined. They made the mistake of banking on the big sale. I have seen this happen countless times to inexperienced reps. You should avoid this trap.

Conversely, the successful sales professional who lands the opportunity of a big account will continue to go on prospecting to develop new business. They will keep the knowledge of this big potential sale in mind, but still will keep working hard to develop new business.

Now if that big sale comes in, that is great and the rep ends up having a fantastic month because there is other business to add to that figure. However, if the big sale does not come through, everything is still okay, because they have managed to develop other business during that month. All hope is not made or lost with one deal.

11. *Don't sound like a cheesy or canned salesperson and don't "show up and throw up!"* Keep your meetings and phone calls conversational and friendly. This approach will help you develop trust for the long term. Think of the definition of what makes a good actor. A good actor is someone who is acting but you can't tell they are acting. They become believable characters because they act true to real life.

The same is true with selling; you need to act natural and not sound like you are selling. You should sound like you are having general conversation that you would have with a friend every day. The more genuine and honest you sound, the better your success ratio.

Also don't "show up and throw up." Many poor salespeople will be so excited about their product that they show up and then "throw up" all of their product's features and benefits to their business prospects without knowing which features and benefits are important to that potential client. The best sales professionals first conduct a needs analysis. What's in it for me? is what every prospect wants to know. Do not start off by pitching the product; learn a little bit about each prospect. Start by asking questions and getting their input and feedback about their experience.

What we have to offer the prospects by selling them tickets is that they will be saving time (tickets are already in hand), saving money (all of our ticket packages are designed to save people money), and they will have great seat locations. Although a stadium might have 80,000 seats, no stadium has 80,000 midfield, front-row, or seats near the team benches. As a sales rep, you will most likely have the best seat locations to sell, which is a wonderful benefit to offer.

A needs analysis is an important part of the sales process. Before you begin any sales presentation, you need to ask questions to learn about your prospect's needs and wants so you will learn what is the most important thing to them.

Good sales professionals will start off a meeting by saying, "Before I tell you about all the great benefits and features of our products, I'd like to start by asking you a few questions about you and your business objectives and needs."

By asking quality questions, you will be able to make more sound recommendations and highlight the features and benefits that are most interesting to your prospect. When you show up and throw up all the benefits, you run the risk of telling the prospect things about your product that they are not interested in.

What if, for example, you were so excited about the free parking pass that was included with the season ticket package that you went on and on about the free parking pass option.

Meanwhile, your prospect doesn't have a car and takes public transportation to the game. Therefore, the prospect doesn't care about the free parking pass. If you had conducted a needs analysis, you would have learned this. However, if you never took the time to learn their needs, you would not have discovered this until it was too late and you spent time talking about a feature that had no importance to your prospect–wasting both of your time.

12. *Attend networking events.* As a rep starting off in the ticket sales business, you should attend as many networking events as possible. You will meet more qualified prospects in a matter of two hours than you will if you make cold calls all day long.

Working for a professional sports team, you have an advantage over selling in other industries. At networking events, people will want to talk to you because people would almost always rather talk about sports than any other industry. At almost every event I attend, the conversation usually turns to a discussion about my team or sports in general.

My co-workers and I often joke about what a great advantage this is when attending networking events. Even working for Major League Soccer where awareness is still relatively low compared to other sports, the conversation always turns to my team. Imagine working for the NFL, the NBA, MLB, or the NHL. When I worked for the NBA, it was the same phenomena. Think about it. What would most people rather talk about: insurance, copiers, law, or professional sports?

Professional networking events are actually something that most pro sports teams don't take enough advantage of. I remember once when I was working for DC United in Washington, D.C., we attended a networking event at the MCI Center, home of the Capitals and Wizards. We had three sales reps at this event and the Wizards and Capitals had no one. We made strong corporate contacts at the event that day that turned into business for our team. This was a big lost opportunity for the Capitals and the Wizards because by not attending they, of course, did not sell one ticket!

When attending networking events, actually work the room and meet contacts. Make the extra effort worth your while. Do not sit around with a co-worker eating and drinking. You can spend two quality hours meeting ten new contacts or you can spend four hours hanging with co-workers making zero contacts. My suggestion is to work the room first to meet prospects, then have fun the last hour of the event.

13. *Develop a plan, implement your plan, and set goals.* Another over-used cliché in business is the one that states, "Most people don't plan on failing, they simply fail to plan." Although you've probably heard this saying a million times, it holds true, especially in the sales profession. The best sales professionals will develop a solid sales plan, and then will implement it. Developing a good plan will help you set your goals, which is also critical to sales success.

A good sales plan will start off by asking a simple question: How much money do you want to make in the upcoming calendar year? Then, using your compensation structure, you need to figure out how much you have to sell in order to earn the desired end-of-year income.

With this figure, you must decide where these sales will come. How many season tickets, group tickets, holiday packages, smaller plans, corporate tickets, and so forth will you need to sell in order to hit your revenue projections? Be sure to make your plan aggressive, but also attainable. It would be foolish to develop a plan that is too easy, however, at the same time it would be professional suicide to develop a plan that is totally unattainable. An unattainable plan would become demotivating over time.

Once you have developed the goals in your plan, you should then develop a timeline to help you stay on track implementing your plan.

You should also set goals for sales activity. First, you should start with setting goals for the number of calls, number of faxes, number of personalized e-mails, and the number of follow-up calls you plan to make every day. You should also set goals for the number of appointments and meetings you intend to have as well as the networking events you plan to attend per week. Set quality sales activity goals for starters, then your sales goals will follow. Learning how to set goals right from the start will help you be successful in sales!

You should work with your sales manager to help you develop your personal sales plan. Your team should also have a ticket sales plan, so your director of sales can help you make sure your personal plan is in line with the team's overall business plan.

14. *Build on your strengths, and strengthen your weaknesses.*

Every sales professional has strengths and weakness. Another critical aspect of having sales success is to first identify what your strengths and weaknesses are. Some sales reps, for example, might be very good at face-to-face meetings, but very poor on the phones trying to book meetings. Other reps might do very well in corporate sales, however, they might struggle with group sales to community groups.

Once you identify your strengths and weaknesses, you can work on maximizing your strengths while strengthening your weaknesses. If you know that you are good in face-to-face meetings, the way you maximize this strength would be to book more meetings. Also, once you have identified your weaknesses, you know where to focus your sales training. For example, if managing the phones properly is a weakness, then seek sales training on developing your phone skills. This can ultimately help you overcome your weaknesses.

15. *Last but not least, have fun and remember you are selling entertainment.* Not to take anything away from other sales industries but always remember that when you are selling tickets for a sports team, you are not selling insurance, copiers, or investments. You are selling entertainment, which means you are selling fun and a chance for people to have an escape from their everyday lives.

You should take advantage of the fact you are selling for a professional sports team. You can invite prospects out to games, meet-the-team events, and team practice sessions. You can also send them team merchandise as a thank you for their business or as an icebreaker to get your foot in the door. You are in the entertainment business, so you also should entertain your clients and prospects using your sport.

If you take these fifteen sales tips into account and implement them in your everyday sales life, you will have success. I do not believe there are any major revolutionary sales tips mentioned here; all of them are common sense. However, you would be surprised to learn how few sales professionals actually follow these basic steps. If you follow these basic sales principles, they will lead you down the right path for sales success. You should think about them every day in your life as a ticket sales professional. Remember, follow these tips and reap the rewards of ticket sales success.

Smart Prospecting Tips to Make Your Sales Come Easier

One way to help you succeed in sales is for you to become an expert in prospecting for new business. Based on a target market of focus, there are many ways to prospect for new clients. You want to explore several opportunities to gather information and learn your marketplace. Finding contact names is also a big key to success.

When looking to develop new business, you should look at the following opportunities:

- Industry lists or association guides or chamber of commerce directories. All chambers of commerce publish a business directory and you should become familiar with them.
- Web sites catering to the industry you are attempting to target. Pharmaceutical companies, for example, typically do a lot of business entertaining. Searching Web sites that cater to the pharmaceutical industry will help your efforts.
- Publications and associations that cater to a certain industry. Similar to Web sites, most industries have an as-

sociation that supports the industry. Examples include American Lawyers Associations, Snack Food Association, American Marketing Association, Toastmasters, and so forth. Most associations publish directories and there are usually publications catering to specific industries. You should become familiar with these types of publications.

- Advertisers trying to target a specific industry. If you are targeting the Latino community, for example, you should learn which types of companies are advertising in the Hispanic community. You should look to approach those companies that are trying to attract the target market you are pursuing.

- Networking events and industry meetings. As mentioned previously, attend as many as you can and try to find the decision makers and introduce yourself to them.

- Find places where decision makers and young professionals gather. Every city in the country has popular, trendy places to eat, drink, and socialize. You should go to these places, develop relationships with the general manager or owner, and ask to put up a fish bowl and raffle off tickets so you can capture business cards. You will be amazed at the number of decision makers who will put their business card into a fish bowl to win your team's tickets.

- Create events of your own where the decision makers might be interested in attending. These include wine tastings, guest bartending, and coaches' seminars or forums. These are more opportunities to cater to a prospect interest.

- Use the phone book, Hispanic Yellow Pages, and business Yellow Pages. The obvious should not be overlooked.

- Guest speaking opportunities. Get in front of your target audience at their meetings. Just as important, capture their names. Raffle merchandise or tickets and have attendees fill out a name-capture raffle entry.

- At the stadium. Meet and greet your contacts at the stadium. Greet group leaders, corporate buyers, and volunteers at soccer (or football or baseball) clubs while at the games. Establishing a ritual of visiting your clients during the game will help you meet new contacts.

As a final note, it's important to learn about your prospects' businesses and their business cycles. When do the companies finalize their budgets? When do soccer camps make up their brochures? When do tournaments mail out their registrations? When do law firms plan their summer outings? Knowing the answers to these questions will help you become a smarter sales professional.

CHAPTER 8

Potential Career Paths

The career path you decide to pursue can go in many different directions starting in ticket sales. Once you get your foot in the door and start having sales success, the possibilities are endless and it is up to you to decide which direction to take your sports career. By gaining insight into how a front office works, you will learn which positions might be of interest to you.

You must remain patient, however, when waiting for your opportunity to arise. Most sports teams' front offices are small and upward mobility might not come easily. Those who continue to have sales success and remain patient will have opportunities come their way. You simply must keep the situation in perspective and wait for your break. You will be presented with opportunities.

Of all the entry-level positions within a sports team, starting in the ticket sales department will provide you with the best experience and background for entering other departments within the organization. I believe this for two reasons:

1. The vital skills you gain in learning how to be successful in sales can carry over to other departments. Knowing how to proactively sell and market your product is the key in many positions including marketing, public relations, and community relations.

I have had many operations and marketing people tell me that they wish they had sales experience because they feel it would make them better candidates to advance within their own careers.

2. No other position within the front office interacts with other departments as much as the ticket sales department. Because of this, you can gain some experience with community relations, customer service, ticket operations, marketing, and public relations.

The same cannot be said for positions in other areas of a professional sports team. Those working in other departments, for the most part, focus only on their particular areas and therefore their experience is limited in scope.

Potential Career Paths from Ticket Sales

Remain a Ticket Sales Representative

Remaining a ticket sales professional might sound obvious. There are many people who have stayed as a ticket sales representative for years and some even remain in ticket sales throughout their entire professional sports career.

As successful sales reps build their base of clients, compensation increases every year. As business relationships develop, their book of business continues to grow. Finding new clients becomes easier. When you have a large base of loyal clients, they will be more likely to pass referrals on to you. Veteran sales reps also enjoy the autonomy of their job; they can often work more flexible hours and they make more money every year. While there is always pressure to produce sales results, there is not as much pressure as those in management have. Therefore, some sales professionals choose to remain in sales and not pursue other opportunities or take on a management role.

Sales Management

If you are successful in ticket sales and have management skills, the next natural transition will be to go into sales management. Successful sales reps can usually master the skill of selling tickets within three to four selling seasons. By gaining sales experience, you will also gain credibility as a sales director.

Managing people, however, is a different skill set than selling. Great salespeople do not always make the best managers. However, all sales directors must know how to sell to be successful. Being promoted to ticket sales director is a goal many sales professionals have. It was my goal when I was selling tickets because I always knew I could be successful as a sales manager.

Sales management has many challenges, but it also has many rewards. If you become a director of sales, it becomes your opportunity to take all the things learned from being in sales and apply it to an entire department. It is also a chance to teach young reps how to be successful in the business. Plus, you are still involved with sales and will always be involved in the appealing aspects of sales.

There is more pressure, however, because as the director of sales you are under the gun for your entire sales team to perform. With added management responsibilities, comes pressure for your sales team to perform. When you are selling tickets as a sales representative, you are only responsible for your own personal sales. However, when you are the director, you are responsible for the entire sales team. If three of your reps perform well, but five fail and you miss your numbers as a result, you are ultimately responsible for the team's overall failure.

Sponsorship Sales

Another natural transition would be to go into business-to-business sponsorship sales. Sponsorship sales is similar to ticket sales in that all the basic selling skills are needed. However, sponsorships sales has higher dollars per transaction. Sponsorships sales involve many marketing and advertising elements which include stadium signage, TV advertising, radio advertising, branding and other in stadium corporate exposure for their logos and brands. For example, Pepsi is a major sponsor of Major League Soccer. As a sponsor, Pepsi has gained marketing rights with all of the teams. They have invested a lot of money in MLS to be the exclusive sponsor of the soft drink category. Therefore, as the official sponsor of MLS, Pepsi gets logo exposure on the field boards in the stadiums, in advertising magazines, on team Web sites, and on teams' TV broadcasts. They also have access to MLS players to use at community events and on commercials. As the official sponsor of Major League Soccer, they also can use MLS logos on all of their packaging.

The sponsorship sales cycle is typically longer than ticket sales. It can take several months and possibly even up to a year to close a sponsor sale, whereas a ticket sale can be closed during the first meeting.

Also, because each sale is a higher dollar value, fewer sponsorship accounts are sold versus ticket accounts. Ticket sales is a volume business with lower dollars per transaction, while sponsorship sales are higher dollars per sale with fewer transactions.

You can make the transition into sponsorship sales if you can master the art selling tickets. If you go into sponsorship sales, you will learn one more valuable part of the business that can make you very marketable in advancing your career.

One might argue that you need to be more "creative" to sell sponsorships, because there can be many elements to a sponsorship sale. However, I feel that if you listen to what a prospective client is looking for and know the assets of what you are selling, you can be successful selling sponsorships.

Other Positions Within Your Team

By starting off in ticket sales, you can also make the transition into other positions within your team. If you have good strong writing skills, you might be able to transition into public relations. Although selling tickets is probably not the most direct route to help you land in a job in PR, you can make the transition if you are already a proven sales commodity. In the end, the PR director must be able to build and maintain strong relationships with members of the media. In ticket sales, you must build strong relationships with your customers.

Ticket sales will teach you how to be "proactive" in order to get more sales. If you took a similar proactive approach to get additional media exposure, this would be invaluable to your team. With the number of sports teams growing in this country, there is a great deal of competition for media coverage.

Securing additional PR for your team can be challenging but can be done using proven sales techniques. I am convinced that if you approach PR similar to how you would approach ticket sale, you will greatly increase the amount of media coverage for your team. The skills you learn in sales will prove to be very favorable if you decide public relations is a career path you would like to pursue.

You can also make the transition into a marketing role. Knowing all of the sales aspects, you will learn how best to market your team. By being on the "front lines" in ticket sales, you will hear what your customers think about your team in the marketplace. Gaining this knowledge will help you make good decisions deciding how to best position your team in the marketplace from a marketing perspective.

Opportunities with Other Teams

The final opportunity that exists when starting off in ticket sales would be to take a position with another sports team. Since many teams' front offices are relatively small, opportunities for promotions internally may not be all that great. Which is why people in professional sports must remain patient when looking to get the next position. Opportunities will not come every day, but they do come if you hang in and continue to do a good job selling tickets.

A reality of being in professional sports is that you might have to relocate several times if you are looking to further your career within the industry. I know several sports executives that have relocated three or four times in order to take promotions or advance their salaries. This is something that you must consider if you want to stay in sports for the long term.

Since advancement within the industry might come from other teams, it is important that you keep your eyes and ears open for opportunities that might exist. It is a good idea to develop relationships with other sales reps working for other teams in your league, as well as perhaps other leagues.

It is also good to inform organizations such as Teamwork that you are looking for new open jobs in sports. Remember, most sports positions will not be advertised anywhere, which means you must keep up to date on positions that are open with other teams. It is not always easy learning of open positions. However, if you develop good relationships within the industry, you will hear of them. Also, if you do a great job for your current team, your managers might recommend you to other teams.

Many top executives communicate with each other and ask for advice when looking to fill positions. You will have opportunities come your way, and you will know when one comes along that will be the right fit for you. You must be prepared to move often if staying in sports is a goal of yours.

The Sky's the Limit!

In the end, you can grow into any position within a sports organization from starting in ticket sales. Whatever career path you decide to pursue, a ticket sales career will give you the necessary background to be successful in professional sports. Mastering the profession of sales can springboard your professional sports career into any direction you wish to take it.

The sky is the limit and it is up to you to take your career as far as you can go or want to go. Growing into upper management is a very realistic opportunity. From the director's position you can grow into a vice president role. Many teams have VP's of sales and marketing and executive vice presidents who oversee all of the team's sales and marketing. These positions are typically the final step to becoming general managers of a team.

Many team presidents and general managers got their career start in ticket sales or as sales professionals in another industry. Nick Sakiewicz, president of the MetroStars, started his career as a sales professional. Tim Leiweike, the current president of the Anschutz Entertainment Group, one of the world's leading companies in live sports and entertainment, got his career start in ticket sales. You too can take your career as far as you can take it. Break into sports through ticket sales and then take your career to the highest possible level!

CHAPTER 9

What Is Marketing, Public Relations, and Community Relations?

"I want to be in marketing, public relations, or community relations."

I can't tell you how many times I have heard this from applicants right out of college looking to land a job in professional sports. Countless times I have heard, "I'll do anything to get my foot in the door, but I really want to be in marketing."

Most candidates think they want to be in these three areas of a sports team. However, when you ask them to describe what these jobs entail, most have no idea. I have received answers like, "I want to promote the sport," or "I want to create ideas to help market the team," or "I want to develop programs and work with companies to do on-field promotions." All of these are perceived "glamorous" sports jobs, but no one ever says, "I want to sell!" Actually, if you ask them if they want to be in ticket sales, most of them will tell you "no." However, they have no idea what they are saying "no" to. Most of the things they describe as aspects of marketing, PR and CR are actually aspects of ticket sales. They just don't know it.

I, too, used to think that I wanted to be in those positions and not in ticket sales. When I first started in ticket sales, I thought that those positions were superior. However, now that I've been in sales and on the revenue-generating side of the business for so long, I can honestly say that I would prefer to be involved with the other areas of the business only in a managerial role.

From my experience in sales, I know that I can do most, if not all, of those jobs. However, not many people in those positions can say the same thing about sales because they have never sold before. Through my sales experience, I now see how my personality, drive, desire, and competitive nature make those jobs not as exciting. In my opinion, they are "safer" jobs with little rejection that must be faced day to day.

Not to take anything away from professionals in any of those positions, but I believe it takes a great deal of courage, perseverance, strength, and commitment to be successful in sales. You need to be bold, put your neck on the line, and face rejection and difficult situations day in and day out.

Learning how to sell and how to be proactive is valuable in any position in the sports business. Too many PR, marketing, and CR managers are simply "reactive"; dealing mostly with issues that come to them. As a result, there is a potential for missed opportunities, selling both themselves and the company short.

There are positive as well as negative aspects about every position in professional sports. Since this book is primarily about ticket sales, this chapter will simply touch on these other opportunities for comparison's sake.

Marketing

Marketing is an ambiguous term that most job candidates cannot define. There are, of course, marketing positions within professional sports teams. Depending on the team and the size of the front office will determine how many marketing positions are available. Teams with small office staffs might have only four or five marketing positions. Larger offices might have an entire marketing department with a much larger staff. Most of the time, however, there are very few entry-level marketing jobs.

Marketing positions are usually filled from within the organization, typically by interns who have proven themselves to the team. People who have previous sports marketing experience with a team or a sports agency are also frequently considered for the marketing department. Occasionally, teams will hire from outside the professional sports arena, most commonly those who have some previous marketing experience. It seems most people who do not have sports marketing experience, come from advertising agencies.

The marketing department is important within a sports team. Effective marketing can help make the ticket sales representative's job easier by supporting them with good general market support for their programs. Some aspects of working in the marketing department include, but are not limited to:

1. Creating advertising messages and campaigns to the general market, possibly working with an outside advertising agency that has been hired by the team.
2. Placing print, radio, and TV advertising in the local market.
3. Creating collateral material for ticketing brochures and other team marketing programs.
4. Overseeing team Web site content and design.
5. Planning direct mail campaigns.
6. Assisting and planning grassroots marketing efforts such as community appearances and mobile marketing vehicle appearances.
7. Fulfilling collateral material and marketing support material requests.
8. Overseeing team merchandise ordering and sales.
9. Working closely with the ticket sales department to provide marketing support for group sales efforts, themed group days, and other community sales efforts.
10. Developing game presentations from scoreboard messages to in-stadium public announcements, in-stadium music, to pregame, half-time, and post-game entertainment.
11. Assisting the sponsorship department in fulfilling sponsorship in game deliverables of pre-game or half time events.

12. Working with donation requests, player appearances, and philanthropic work (in the event community relations falls under the marketing department).

Marketing positions are good jobs and those professionals fortunate enough to land one should feel grateful. Being involved in the creative aspects of the job, such as having responsibility for the overall team image and branding, can be appealing. Although you can be creative in a ticket sales position, a marketing position requires a lot of creativity, especially when charged with designing general advertising themes and marketing messages that will be used in all of the team's advertising campaigns. Ticket sales professionals will have a lot of input in this area as well, however, the marketing department is ultimately responsible for the team's overall marketing message taken to the community.

When you are in marketing, you are effectively on the buyer side of the business, because the marketing department typically negotiates with media advertising outlets. Being on the buyer side of the business can gratifying, especially when you are the one being "schmoozed" by all of your advertising partners. In sales, you are the one doing the "schmoozing" of your prospects and clients. In marketing, because you are the one being sold, you must determine how to best spend your advertising dollars. While this is a positive part of the business, it can also be annoying. I know many marketing mangers who complain about being bombarded by sales people who constantly call, trying to sell them advertising.

The marketing and ticket sales departments often work very closely together. The most successful sports organizations make sure the marketing department and sales department communicate with each other and are on the same page when developing their business plans. This makes sense since marketing campaigns work to drive business to the sports teams in the way of Web site sales, incoming ticket sales phone calls, walk-up ticket sales, and outlet ticket sales to the general market. A successful marketing campaign can help increase ticket sales and make ticket sales efforts easier.

Although it is certainly an important part of the professional sports business, there are challenges to being in marketing.

Earning potential can be somewhat limited. The director of marketing position is usually based on a straight salary with limited bonus or commission opportunities. The base salaries of some entry marketing positions are also relatively low. While the base salaries may be higher than those in ticket sales, factoring in potential bonus and commissions that ticket sales reps can earn, final compensation is often much higher for ticket sales professionals.

Being in marketing can often be frustrating, because many times it is difficult to have measurable results from marketing activities. For example, results from an advertisement that has run in a local newspaper may be difficult to track. It is also tough to track the results of a television campaign or a billboard advertising campaign. Unless there is a specific call to action or a specific promotion advertised in one advertising medium, results might be difficult to measure. Furthermore, some marketing initiatives are put in place to help brand the team and bring awareness to the team instead of directly trying to impact ticket sales. It can be very difficult to gauge the impact of this branding-type of advertising.

Marketing initiatives are also often at the mercy of elements that are out of your control. The weather, economy, competition in the marketplace, and poor team performance are all things that you cannot control and can lead to less than desirable results.

For example, you might have a great advertising strategy with fantastic ad placements, but your target audience still might decide not to purchase tickets or attend a team event. Or you may have a great campaign for a game, only to have it rain or snow right before game time, which results in fans staying home. These are frustrating factors over which the marketing manager must face from time to time.

In ticket sales, however, while these mentioned factors make it more difficult to sell, there is usually a cure: You can always pick up the phone and make one more call, go on one more sales appointment, or attend one more networking event.

You have more control over your success when you are in ticket sales. Marketing initiatives are put out into the community, and then must wait for the buying community to react, whereas ticket sales take the sales message to the community where you can convince a prospect to buy in a direct sales environment.

Marketing positions are very good positions within a professional sports team. However, they are not easy to acquire. It is possible to make the transition from ticket sales to the marketing department. Having ticket sales experience would be good to have if presented with the challenge of marketing a team. You will have a better understanding as to what it takes to sell tickets. Furthermore, marketing and ticket sales are very closely related, probably more so than most people think. Good sports organizations will ensure that marketing and sales work closely together to achieve the team's business objectives.

Public Relations

Similar to teams' marketing departments, the size of the team and the league office will determine how many PR positions there are. PR positions require individuals who have strong written and verbal communication skills. Compensation for working in the PR department is typically straight-base salary. Entry-level PR positions often start at the bottom of the pay scale in a professional sports office. Most PR professionals get their career start from internships in media relations.

Some duties of the PR department include, but are not limited to:

1. Working with mainstream sports media and team beat writers, developing strong relationships with each.
2. Producing timely press releases about team-related news item: player transactions, trades, and game information.
3. Attempting to get non-traditional sports media placed for the team, such as working with all types of media outlets to try and coverage for the team and players.

Non-traditional sports media includes magazines, newspapers, and TV shows that don't have anything to do with sports. Examples of this would be having an article about a player in the Style section of the paper instead of the sports pages. Or having a player on *Entertainment Tonight* instead of on ESPN.

4. Working with the players and coaches to field interview requests from the media.
5. Setting up media days, luncheons, and other media relationship building events.
6. Setting up press conferences for major team announcements.
7. Writing material for the media guide including team information and player biographies.
8. Helping get coverage for local community events and player appearances in smaller town papers.
9. Talking daily with the media and handling all media inquiries from teams' beat writers.
10. Working with the media on game days to make sure they have game notes, proper credentials, and are treated first class so they will leave with a favorable impression of the team.

One attractive aspect of PR is that it is typically easier than sales to find who your customers are. There is always some interest in every sports team from a handful of beat writers. Beat writers are assigned from major publications to cover all of the various professional sports teams. This means that you automatically know who your "customers" are while in sales you often have to go out and find your customers. It is important to be good at establishing and maintaining relationships with writers whose job it is to cover your team. More established sports such as the NBA, NFL and MLB often have many beat writers assigned from all the major local newspapers and TV stations. The more popular the team, the more media members follow and are assigned to cover the team.

Another attractive aspect about PR is the fact that you are around the team a good percentage of the time. As a result, you can establish personal relationships with the players. You also get invited to industry events where there are other sports celebrities. Thus, you are exposed to the more "glamorous" side of the business. You also have some exposure to the team while in ticket sales, however not to the degree as those in PR.

Finally, many PR directors travel with, and are considered to be, part of the team. Most sports teams have one or several members of the PR staff travel to attend to the needs of media members at away games. PR directors travel in order to produce timely information from the games. For many, this is an extremely attractive element of the job.

One thing to keep in mind about PR, however, is that PR representatives work very long hours on game days. They typically have to get to the stadium hours before game time to prepare for all aspects of the media's needs.

They also have to stay until after the game is finished to prepare press releases and games notes for distribution to the sports wires. Many PR people are in charge of updating content on the team's Web site as well as conduct postgame player and coach interviews. Because the PR department is usually the first to the stadium, and the last to leave the stadium, they do a lot of grueling behind-the-scenes work that often goes unnoticed. Most of what they report on are all things that happened within the game itself. Therefore, many PR people love the sports they are working for, so much so that I consider many to be the ultimate fans of the team.

I have one final comment about public relations positions as it relates to this book. There is a distinction in my opinion between public relations and media relations. I would classify most of the PR people that I have encountered working in professional sports as media relations and not public relations. The difference between media relations and public relations is that media relations can be looked at as more of a customer service position, where as public relations is more similar to a sales position.

The reason I would define media relations as a position very similar to customer service is that media relations focuses on catering to the needs of the media who are interested in the team; essentially, the team's media customers. I would say public relations is more in line with sales, in that true public relations has to do with finding proactive new ways to increase media exposure above and beyond the opportunities that typically come to teams.

Most of the PR people that I've encountered do not have a sales background; therefore, they become good at dealing with the media that comes to them and good at customer service. However, I do not believe they are very good at seeking new and creative ways to reach the public and maximize exposure. Meaning, they are not very good at media sales.

In some of the most popular sports teams around the country, good media relations is a critical to the success of the team. The New York Yankees, for example, have a large amount of media interest in their team. So much interest, in fact, that they have the luxury of being selective in regards to the media outlets with which they work. They also must be protective of their players, since too many people want access to them. Due to the high interest in the team and large volume of demand, they must be selective as to which media outlets gain access to the team and their players.

However, teams like the Yankees are the exception and not the rule in sports these days. Most professional sports teams can use more positive media pick-up and exposure for the team and its players.

In my opinion, that is the downfall of the way some teams treat and look at their PR departments. I believe that if teams' PR departments focused on being more public relations focused instead of media relations focused, they would be more successful at maximizing media opportunities. This would help with a team's overall success.

If they applied simple sales principles to their jobs, they would uncover many untapped opportunities for additional publicity for their respective teams. By being proactive in the community, paying attention to nontraditional media, local publications, and numerous radio station outlets, they could tap into additional incremental PR opportunities.

Often PR people function in a bubble and are surrounded by people who have an interest in the team. As a result, they are not often as proactive as they possibly could be, therefore missing potential opportunities for the team.

In summary, although PR may be attractive to a lot of people coming into the field of sports, you must to be prepared of some of the negative aspects associated with it, in particular the hours required. I feel starting off in sales and transitioning into public relations could be a good route to take, especially if you have good communication skills. If more PR people could apply basic sales principals to their jobs, they would be more effective. This is why more teams should consider transitioning ticket sales people into PR—they may have more overall success.

Community Relations

Community relations departments deal with the various entities in the community who look to associate themselves with a professional sports team. The community relations department also usually works with the players for nonmedia-type events and appearances. The community relations department and media relations department should work closely together. They should also work closely with the ticket sales department as well, since many ticket sales relationships offer both community relations opportunities as well as PR opportunities.

Some of the community relations department's duties include, but are not limited to:

1. Working with charity groups, schoo ls, and other groups and organizations looking to associate themselves with the team.
2. Handling donation requests from various organizations for fundraising, silent auctions, raffles, and other outlets.
3. Working with players to book player appearances in the community.
4. Working with other charitable organizations such as children's hospitals to book additional player appearances for nonprofit groups.
5. Helping organize and coordinate community events.
6. Working with the marketing department to maximize grassroots marketing efforts.

Several positives exist for a position in community relations. For starters, like public relations, people in community relations get to interact with the players, often building strong relationships with them. Many people enjoy this part of the business, another perceived "glamorous" part of the sports business. Having a working relationship with professional athletes and getting to know them on a personal basis can be a perceived privilege of the job.

Working with a wide variety of charitable groups and organizations allows the team an opportunity to give back to the community. Building meaningful relationships with charities that have a positive impact in the community can be extremely rewarding. It is also rewarding to see a team's players have an impact on a terminally ill child or helping organizations such as the Susan G. Komen Foundation raise thousands of dollars to help fight breast cancer.

CR is typically a lower-pressure job than being in ticket sales, since the pressure to produce sales results is not there every day. There is certainly hard work and many long hours are also required. However, there isn't the same amount of pressure to hit revenue goals, sales targets, or drive in sales. Many CR representatives feel overworked and underappreciated because their time is in demand as in almost any professional sports job, but there aren't always measurable results as there are in other positions. Consequently, the department is looked at more as a cost center than a profit center, which means sometimes teams might question whether or not having community relations is justifiable.

While working with the players can be seen as a positive, it can also be a negative. Many CR representatives learn that professional athletes can be difficult to work with. Generally speaking, the more money athletes make, the more popular they become, the more public interest they receive, and the more difficult they can be to work with. Professional athletes are often "babied" by teams, their agents, general managers, and the media. They get used to this treatment and become high maintenance, which can often make them difficult to work with.

Consequently, many CR managers begin to recognize these athletes are simply people like everyone else. Although there are players with great personalities who are easy to work with, there are also those who are "prima donnas" and want everything handed to them on a silver platter. Thus, this job requires a lot of patience and an ability to win over the trust of players in order to get them to attend appearances and other requirements as needed.

There are usually few positions in the community relations department of sports teams, with compensation typically on the low side with a base salary only.

Finally, while CR managers do interact with other departments within the organization, they are not involved all that much with planning or creating business plans. They simply tend to implement programs and deal with the community on a grass roots level.

CHAPTER 10

Useful Information to Help You Land a Job in Sports

There are a few companies, Web sites, and books that I would recommend researching prior to pursuing a career in professional ticket sales. Although not many entities are dedicated to ticket sales as a profession, there are a few and some that I feel are better than the rest. Additionally, I have personal experiences with many and would strongly endorse those recommended in this chapter. In no particular order, following are resources worth investigating on your own.

Game Face Marketing

Based in Portland, Oregon, and run by Rob Cornilius, Game Face began as a ticket sales training company and has now transformed into a ticket sales training academy or "boot camp."

Rob got his start as a ticket sales representative for the Los Angeles Clippers. The Clippers traditionally were at the bottom of the NBA in attendance. Poor team performance and lack of recognition made selling tickets to the Clippers extremely challenging. Rob, however, successfully developed a ticket sales strategy, which helped him sell tickets to a team that no one wanted to buy.

Rob recognized that although there were many companies that specialized in sales training, there were none that specialized in professional sports ticket sales training. Thus, he launched Game Face Marketing and developed a two-day ticket sales training seminar. Several trainers, as well as Rob himself, visit teams who hire his firm to come and train their sales staffs.

The training seminar is based on successful techniques and steps that he followed when selling tickets for the Clippers. Many professional sports teams have used Game Face Marketing to train their ticket sales teams and as a result, his company has trained probably thousands of ticket sales professionals throughout the United States and around the world.

Game Face Marketing's new ticket sales academy is designed to provide intense training to candidates looking to break into sports through ticket sales. Trainees conduct advanced training individually at home and then go to Portland for several weeks of training and on the job sales work. I have hired several candidates from the Game Face Marketing Academy and they have all performed well.

If you were serious about a career in ticket sales, investing time and money to attend the Game Face Marketing Academy is recommended. They also have a professional recruitment division who helps academy graduates land jobs with professional sports teams.

Since Game Face has worked with many professional sports team, their professional recruitment division is very effective. They have developed strong relationships with many directors of sales for a lot of teams and have a very high success rate for placing their graduates.

A slight word of caution, however, about using their recruitment services. Game Face Marketing charges a finder's fee to teams if they want to hire one of their candidates. Which means that you are now a candidate with a finder's fee attached to you. This can work against you.

Many teams are accustomed to paying finder's fees to placement companies for executive positions; however, they are sometimes not able to justify placement fees for entry-level ticket sales candidates. Therefore, while they will help you get more interviews with teams, this association might also prevent some teams from being able to hire you. This is simply something to consider, however, I would recommend attending the

Game Face Marketing Academy or at the least investigating them for yourself.

Game Face, Inc., Headquarters
19125 SW 125th Ct.
Tualatin, OR 97062
Phone: 503.692.8855
Fax: 503.692.8866
www.gamefacemarketing.com

TeamWork Online LLC.

Founded in 1987, Team Work Online is designed to help professional sports team employers find candidates who want to work in professional sports. Although they do not specialize in ticket sales, they do help many teams fill ticket sales positions. They have served over 120 sports and sports-related organizations and recruited over 325 individuals, averaging about 40 completed searches a year.

Team Work Online is also a sports executive search firm. The following is the company description from the Team Work Online Web site:

> *Team Work Online is a retained executive search firm. Our focus is recruiting executives for mid- to senior-level positions in the sports and live-event industry. We have recruited more executives into the sports and live-event industry than any other executive search firms.*

As a job seeker, you should go to this Web site and post your resume for jobs that interest you. You are certain to find a lot of teams hiring ticket sales professionals on this Web site. You might also want to contact Team Work Consulting directly and ask them for advice on how to properly post your resume and cover letter. Tell them the kind of ticket sales jobs you are interested in, because the staff at Team Work knows of recruiters' needs for many teams in sports.

Team Work is also the best in the business in terms of communicating directly with hiring managers at professional sports teams. They often have a dedicated representative assigned to each team and that person communicates frequently with the recruiting managers. Being a busy business executive, I am impressed with the diligent follow up and customer service that I receive from TeamWork Online.

I have worked with other online recruiters and no other company has followed up as thoroughly as Team Work Online. Therefore, I usually end up interviewing candidates from the Team Work Web site and most of my hirings are Team Work Online candidates.

If you decide to post your resume on the Team Work Web site, I would suggest that you take advantage of all their options on the page:

1. **Post your resume.** There is an option for you to attach and post your resume. I am always shocked at the number of candidates who do not post their resumes. Actually, most candidates don't post much information at all. This is a huge mistake because I rarely look further at these candidates. How can a recruiting manger look closely at candidates when no additional relevant information exists about the candidates? It makes no sense for a candidate to reply to a job posting and offer no additional information. I never contact candidates who don't attach their resumes.

2. **Post a specific cover letter for the job for which you are posting.** Once again, I am amazed at the number of candidates who do not take advantage of the opportunity to post a cover letter as well. Also, some candidates post a generic cover letter instead of a specific cover letter for the job for which they are applying. Even if you are applying for a number of jobs, it is in your best interest to take a few extra minutes and customize the cover letter for the position for which you are applying. This will help you stand out from the rest of the candidates.

3. **Contact the employer via e-mail or phone.** I would always recommend that candidates make a personal contact to the teams of the jobs that you are interested in. Some of my job postings have as many as 300 candidates responding to our openings. There is a chance that I may miss a qualified candidate simply because of the volume of candidates. You need to contact the employer and express your interest in the job.

Hopefully these tips will help you better utilize their Web site. The teamwork staff does an excellent job communicating with the teams and helping teams fill vacant positions. My personal experiences with TeamWork Online have all been very positive and I use them more than any other recruiting service. I strongly recommend their services to any candidate.

Team Work Online LLC.
22550 McCauley Road
Shaker Heights, OH 44122
Phone: 216. 360-1790
info@teamworkonline.com
Web site: www.teamworkonline.com

Additional Professional Recruiting Firms

More companies that you can investigate to help you land a job include:

Women in Sports Careers Foundation

The mission of the Women in Sports Careers Foundation is to provide women professional guidance, education, and support to pursue and manage sports-related careers. WISC Foundation services include career educations, seminars and an internship program.

Women In Sports Careers Foundation
Phone: (714) 848-1201

support@wiscfoundation.org
www.wiscfoundation.org

WomenSportsJobs.com

WomenSportsJobs.com is one of the leading online career center for women in the sports industry, and for women interested in sports related fields. They provide their members the opportunity to search hundreds of jobs in the sports industry, while providing employers an opportunity to search a pool of qualified and diversified candidates.

Women's Sports Jobs is a paid service for both job seekers and employers. Job seekers can join on an annual basis or on a monthly basis. Annual Membership fees are around $100 and monthly fee's around $20. They also have resume review and resume writing services. While they primarily support women looking to land a job in sports, they also have services for men.

Women's Sports Jobs
Phone: (714) 848-1201
jobs@womensportsjobs.com
www.womensportsjobs.com

General Sports and Entertainment

General Sports is a multifaceted sports and entertainment firm that includes Executive Placement along with other services they provide to the sports industry. While they typically recruit executive level candidates, they will also help ticket sales candidates and other entry level candidates as well. Along with Executive Placement their other services include, Consulting Services, Hospitality and Event Management, Naming Rights and Sponsorship and Team Acquisitions.

The mission of General Sports and Entertainment is to use the power of sports and entertainment to help their clients build relationships with other clients, customers, employees, and their community. Their objective is to help clients increase profits and grow their business.

General Sports & Entertainment
400 Water Street
Suite 250
Rochester, Michigan 48307
Phone: (248) 601-2200
www.generalsports.com

Work in Sports

Work in Sports is the premiere sports employment resource providing members access to hundreds of current sports jobs and internships. Members can also post resumes and search contact information for hundreds of organizations in the highly competitive sports industry. Work in Sports is also a paid service for job seekers with monthly fees around $25.

Work in Sports LLC
7335 East Acoma Drive
Suite 201
Scottsdale AZ 85260
Phone: (480) 905-7221
members@workinsports.com
www.workinsports.com

Professional Baseball Employment Opportunities

PBEO.com is the official Web site of the Minor League Baseball employment service. PBEO.com provides a career network for job seekers looking to gain employment in professional baseball by providing continuous access to Minor League Baseball and Major League Baseball clubs. PBEO is also a paid service with annual membership costing around $50. Members' resumes are placed in their database according to areas of interest, geographical preference and over team interest.

Additional membership benefits include a monthly newsletter, auto—notification of new job openings, articles from member clubs, career tips and information on job fairs and events.

PBEO.com
PO Box A
St. Petersburg, FL 33731
Telephone: (866) 937-7236
memberservice@pbeo.com
www.pbeo.com

Teamjobs.com

Teamjobs.com is another Web site service dedicated to helping people land a job in professional sports. They offer a software product that you can download or order from their website for around $70. The software includes a database of professional teams phone numbers, fax numbers, e-mail address, websites and specific job profiles. I am not all that familiar with this software product. However, I found it on the Internet and thought it was worthy of mention. The Web site is www.teamjobs.com. There is no other information available about this service.

Grip University

"Grip U" is a new service offered by Grip Sales and Service. Grip U is a skill development program designed to prepare serious and aggressive sales and marketing executives ready for full time sales, customer service and marketing positions within the sports, entertainment and corporate industries. Whether you're looking to break into the industry or you're an executive looking for pre-trained sports sales and marketing professionals, Grip U can help.

Only a limited number of the highest quality candidates are admitted for each program and all of the placements are guaranteed by Grip. Grip U graduates are prepared in B2B and B2C business development, sports and entertainment ticket sales, operations, grass roots marketing, events, sponsorship sales, premium and suite sales, customer service and promotions.

While it is a new program offered by Grip, I found Grip's sales training provided by Grip's principal, Bret Pulverosa, to be very solid. You should check out this relatively new company if you would like more personalized sales training.

Grip Sales and Service Training
6502 SE 32nd Avenue
Portland, Oregon 97202
bjp@gripinc.com
www.gripinc.com

Sports Business Books and Publications

Books by John Spoelstra

There are three books by John Spoelstra that I would recommend reading. John is a well-known professional sports author who is credited with writing the first ticket sales book. His books have revolutionized the way professional sports teams sell tickets. His most well known book, *How to Sell the Last Seat in the House,* is probably one of the most acknowledged books in the history of professional sports business.

How to Sell the Last Seat in the House discusses every topic of the ticket sales profession including group sales, individual household sales, corporate sales, pricing strategies and marketing ideas. Today many teams continue to implement many of the ideas that he presented in his book. This book is considered to be the bible of professional sports ticket sales.

In order to read this book, you might have to contact someone within the professional sports industry to obtain a copy. It is a difficult book to find since it retails for around $350. Due to this high price point, many teams own it since it was not produced in mass quantity for individuals. It was priced so teams would purchase copies for their offices.

If you can obtain a copy, and find yourself extremely interested in the content, then you know that a ticket sales career is for you. I personally picked up a copy early in my career and could not put it down the first time I read it. This is another reason why I knew a ticket sales career was for me.

I do not believe that every theory or idea that John has in *How to Sell the Last Seat in the House* is one hundred percent correct. While it is a highly acknowledged book in the sports industry, many professional sports executives discredit his book and his theories, which is unfortunate. Those who don't believe in the book, probably tried one or two of his theories which failed to work and as a result they ended up abandoning all of his practices. Spoelstra's theories are like most ideas; there are so many variables that every idea cannot possibly work for everyone. However, if you read them and then try to apply a few ideas and stay disciplined in seeing the theory through, many are bound to work.

For example, when I was at DC United, we attempted to use his theory for pricing our stadium. Spoelstra believes that the best seats in the house should be available for full-season tickets only and should be priced the highest.

We followed this plan and it backfired on us during the first year. The reason it didn't work is that is that we came to find out that scaling the house works best if you have seating scarcity in an arena. However, we were playing in RFK Stadium which has 50,000 seats and we sold only around 5,000 season tickets. Obviously seat scarcity was not an issue.

Therefore, blocking partial season ticket holders from prime mid-field locations did not make sense for us. The good news is, we quickly learned from our mistake and adjusted accordingly midway through the sales season. Therefore, that particular idea did not work for us, but I'm sure for many professional teams playing in smaller arenas, this theory probably does work and many still implement it today.

You should read *How to Sell the Last Seat in the House* before you begin your professional ticket sales career. The ideas and theories provided within will get your mind thinking the way a ticket sales professional should think. Then you should decide for yourself which practices and theories will work best for your team.

John Spoelstra has also written two other books that I recommend. One is titled *Ice to Eskimos* and the other book is called *Marketing Outrageously*. In *Ice to Eskimos*, Spoelstra takes sports marketing practices and attempts to apply them to the real business world. In *Marketing Outrageously*, he attempts to give business professionals various marketing techniques and ideas to help find new business. I have read all of Spoelstra's books and have found them to be extremely valuable tools in helping me grow as a ticket sales professional.

Books by Pat Williams

Pat Williams has also written two books on the professional sports business. Pat is the current Senior Vice President of the Orlando Magic. Prior to joining the Orlando Magic, he spent time with the Philadelphia 76ers, the Atlanta Hawks and the Chicago Bulls.

His book *The Magic of Teamwork* discusses how by using the power of teamwork, one can lead teams to success both on and off the field. It is a particularly good book to read if you are planning to get into management. His other book is called *Go for the Magic*. Both of his books can be found in most major bookstores across the country.

Sports Business Journal

The *Sport Business Journal* (www.sportsbusinessjournal.com) was launched in April 1998. Each week, the journal provides the critical news and information that sports industry leaders need to compete, negotiate, and succeed in their industry.

Every issue features coverage of the deals, trades, contracts, and boardroom power plays that shape the rapidly changing sports industry. Regular columns cover every aspect of the sports industry from media and marketing to finance and facilities.

Because it is a trade publication, annual subscriptions are around $200, which is expensive as far as magazines go. However, there is no better publication to learn everything there is to know about the sports business and sports-business executives.

Although it seems pricey, if you would like to make a small investment in your future career, subscribing to the *SBJ* will be invaluable to you.

Sports Meetings and Conferences

Many sports marketing conferences, seminars, and annual meetings where sports executives gather are scheduled throughout the year. These meetings provide an excellent opportunity for job candidates to land a job with a professional team. For example, baseball Major League Baseball holds its annual Baseball Winter meetings each off season. Check out www.minorleaguebaseball.com to learn where the Winter Meetings are held each year.

All sports executives from Major League Baseball and Minor League Baseball gather for this weeklong meeting. Many teams actually set up recruiting booths to talk with job candidates. Attending this event will land you in front of many team executives and can help you land a job in the baseball.

Furthermore, there is an annual PBEO job fair that is designed to help job seekers land a job in professional baseball. Go to www.PBEO.com and look for the link for the annual job fair.

Another example of great events to attend would be Major League Soccer championship games or all-star games. At both Major League Soccer events, business meetings accompany the soccer events. All of the teams' general managers, ticket directors, marketing directors, and league officials gather to discuss the business of the sport. Many social activities and parties are thrown, which are great venues for networking if you can find out where the evening-hour events are and then attend.

This event would provide a great opportunity to meet face to face with decision makers who can hire candidates into their teams. Most GM's, Vice Presidents and Directors would be very impressed if a job seeker attended these meetings and made the effort to make a introduction of themselves and asked to speak about job opportunities. They would tell you who you would need to speak with at their respective teams and tell you about their possible opportunities.

Sports Business Journal 40-Under-40 Awards

Every year, the *Sports Business Journal* recognizes the top forty sports executives under 40 years of age. They honor and invite all the winners to their annual awards banquet and dinner. Sports executives are very proud to win this award and the weekend is very well attended.

Attending an event like this would give job seekers a huge advantage in landing a job. While the dinner banquet is a private event on Saturday night, gathered in one hotel for one weekend are all of the brightest sports executives in the business. If you were to go to the hotel during the afternoon or at cocktail hour, you will certainly bump into many of these executives and be able to speak with them. The *Sports Business Journal* Web site will publicize who the Forty under Forty are and with some research you can decide who you want to meet. Not only might you land a job, but you might also learn on how these executives got their career starts and landed their dream job.

Sports Super Show

The final conference I'd like to mention is the Sports Super Show (www.thesupershow.com) It is a conference dedicated to being the premier global event for the growth of sports and fitness. While this is not the best conference to help you land a ticket sales job, it is one of the largest in the Sports Industry which makes it worthy of mention.

Buyers and apparel manufacturers from across the globe network through display booths, private meeting, and presentation rooms as well as corporate parties and receptions. I attended the Super Show for almost three years in the row because I was friends with someone who was a rep for a major shoe manufacturer. The first several days of the show are intended for those in the industry only. The general public is typically invited during the final day.

Every year his company would have a presence because most of their accounts would come and place orders for the year at the Super Show. It is a great place to meet prospective employers especially if you were looking at a job for a big company like Nike, Adidas or Reebok.

While the show is mostly geared towards retail manufactures and buyers, most professional sports leagues have a presence due to licensing of team merchandise. All leagues sell official licensed products at the Super Show and you will be able to walk right up to league representatives and ask them who to contact at teams for potential sales positions

Hopefully I have given you some useful information in this chapter to help you land a job in professional sports. I wish I had this information when I was trying to land a job. However, I learned about most of them as I gained more experience in professional sports.

Please check my Web site, www.breakintosports.com which has links and more information about all contained in this chapter.

CHAPTER 11

Case Studies of Sports Professionals

Most of this book has been about my personal experiences in professional ticket sales. I thought that it would be useful to conclude this book with actual case studies from other professionals in sports business to get their opinions on ticket sales.

I have included several stories from professionals in various sports. One person wished to remain anonymous, but gave me permission to use his thoughts. I hope you find these case studies to be both interesting and valuable.

Case Study 1

Drew Young
Sales Executive
Premium Services
Philadelphia Eagles

How long have you held your current position?

One year with the Philadelphia Eagles

What other professional positions have you held?

Greensboro College: Athletic/Admissions Recruiter; Loudon County Government: Youth Sports Coordinator; DC United: Account Executive, Senior Manager,

Assistant Director of Sales; Adidas World Cup Internship–summer 1995.

How and when did you know you wanted a career in pro sports?

I was working for the county government coordinating their youth sports leagues and I had to listen to some lady who was complaining that her six-year-old did not get the proper sign-up information. She had signed him up for a youth softball league and was complaining about everything. Her son was only six years old and she was taking the recreation program way too seriously. She had me on the phone for 30 minutes, complaining about the problem. I knew at that time I needed to get out of government work and into pro sports.

How did you "break in"? What was your first job in pro sports?

My first "pro sports" job was with DC United of Major League Soccer. It was a sales position with a base salary of around $20,000 a year. On top of my base salary, I had to sell $180,000 worth of tickets in order to hit my draw and make commission. I almost didn't take the job but my wife talked me into it. She said, "This might be your only opportunity to get into pro sports." She knew that I was miserable working outside of sports and that my love of sports would make me happier in this position than I had been. So I accepted the position and worked crazy hours, 8:00 A.M. to 9:00 P.M. Monday through Friday. I tried to talk to everyone that I could about buying tickets from me.

What sacrifices did you make in order to get into pro sports?

When you get into sports everyone says, "Wow, that is a great job you have." Well, it is but you have to make a lot of sacrifices such as long hours and a lot of night and weekend hours at games and events. However, the rewards are great as well. Especially after you start having sales success. You are working in an industry and selling a product that you love. The positives far outweigh the negatives, but it is tough when you first start out.

What risks did you take in order to get into sports?

When I accepted my first professional sports job, my salary went from bad to worse. When you start out in pro sports, your salary is not as good as in other industries. However sales is one of the best and only ways to break into pro sports. Everyone wants a marketing position, or thinks they want a marketing position, but the way to get into sports is to know how to sell. If you know how to sell, you will write your own ticket.

What advice would you give individuals who want to pursue a career in professional sports?

If you want to get into pro sports I would do an internship and ask to be placed in the sales department. Ask to help in anyway you can so you can learn how to sell. Sit in on all meetings, go to all the games, and ask for work. Come in early and stay late . . . that way people in the office, "the higher ups," and the team executives see that you are working hard. You will stand out, be noticed and end up getting a job.

Case Study 2

Marc Steir
Manager
Corporate Ticket Sales
New York Mets Major League Baseball

How long have you held your current position?

Since January 2002, over two years.

What other professional positions have you held?

New York Mets Major League Baseball; Corporate Ticket Sales

New Haven Ravens (AA Eastern League); Director of Group Sales, Merchandise Manager

New Britain Rock Cats (AA Eastern League); Intern, Head Manager

University of Massachusetts Men's Basketball; Student Manager: UMass Men's Basketball

How and when did you know you wanted a career in pro sports?

Reality had set in that I wouldn't be playing second base in the big leagues around eighth grade, but I still could never imagine anything else I would want to do but be involved in sports. It was just a question of figuring out how. Late in my high school career it became clear to me that I wanted to be in the business of sport. I will give it up when it stops being fun.

How did you "break in"? What was your first job in pro sports?

My first experience in sports was as a volunteer student manager for the UMass men's basketball team. My first paying job was as a general intern for the New Britain Rock Cats, Eastern League AA Affiliate of the Minnesota Twins.

What sacrifices did you make in order to get into pro sports?

I did not sacrifice in the same sense that many people are forced to sacrifice financially just to make ends meet. I was fortunate enough to have enough money where I had the luxury to make the choice to work in sports where the starting salary was not what I could have gotten somewhere else. I guess my sacrifices come down to probably the same thing as everyone else: time and money. I spent, and still spend many more hours than a lot of folks do working my hardest to get where I am now. I work this hard in order to get where I am going to go in the future. It is also understood that working in sports is a lower paid industry in comparison to a similar job in another industry, especially in the beginning. This is why you have to really enjoy being in the industry to survive in it.

What risks did you take?

I think my greatest risks have yet to be taken. Probably the biggest to date would be taking a sales job with the New Haven Ravens where more than half my salary would be commission, without having any prior sales experience. That is a scary experience for anyone.

What advice would you give individuals who want to pursue a career in professional sports?

The first thing is to understand what you are getting yourself into, because you are entering an extremely glamorous, enormous revenue-generating industry, in a very unglamorous, low-paying way. If you do not go in with that attitude, you will never be happy working in the industry. The people in this industry—and really in all industries who are unhappy—are the people who have the attitude that something is owed to them. Successful people understand that no one owes them anything; they go out and take it . . . I would try to learn as much as I can at every opportunity I can, remembering that you learn the most by doing and experiencing things as opposed to asking questions and being lectured.

When you are first starting out as an intern or a student, get experience in as many aspects of an organization as you can. This will help you understand everything that goes into running an organization and also give you an appreciation for what others are going through as you move up and become more specialized. No matter what specific part of the business you go into, it will always be a great help to you to get some experience in sales.

Most people don't realize that sales teaches you how to communicate with people and that is a skill that will be of great benefit to you no matter what job you do. Sales is also a great way to break into the industry and probably the best way to advance your career the quickest. The bottom line in any industry will always be money, and if you can prove to people that you can make them money, your value to them will increase exponentially.

Case Study 3

Chris Schiller
Sales Manager
Buffalo Bills, NFL

How long have you held your current position?

Four years working with the Buffalo Bills.

How and when did you know you wanted a career in pro sports?

I have played sports my entire life. I knew right when a sports marketing book was placed in front of me in high school that sports would be the avenue I would take. I have excelled in sports my entire life and love professional sports. I knew it would be the profession for me.

How did you "break into sports?" What was your first job in pro sports?

I broke into a professional sports career because I played professional lacrosse. My current boss heard I was looking for a job and hired me as a sales coordinator. I didn't make enough money playing professional lacrosse and knew I would have to find a job working in the executive offices of a sports team.

What sacrifices did you make in order to get into professional sports?

There were no sacrifices before I got into pro sports. It is the sacrifices you have to make during your career with pro sports—time and money. You are overworked and underpaid when you first start out. However, the longer you have been in it, the more rewards begin to come your way, such as being around the professional game and all the perks that come with it. In the end, you are selling a product that people love and are excited about, instead of selling a product that is difficult to get excited about such as insurance or bug spray.

What risks did you take?

My risk was that I had to leave a job where I made twice as much money as my offer to join the Bills. Plus I had to move out of one career where I had experience, into another where I had no experience. I did not love the first job that I had out of school. I was selling pest control to companies. I was the "bug guy," the guy that came into an office and told you that you had a bug problem. That was not a very glamorous job. We used to laugh and joke about it with my friends. So even though I took a pay cut to move into a sports position, it was an opportunity to trade in a profession that I didn't love for a job that I love.

What advice would you give individuals who want to pursue a career in professional sports?

The absolute bottom line is this: You can never judge or compare how much money you make to how much you love what you are doing. Sports (the majority of the time), in the beginning will not get you rich but what it will do is improve your credibility, accountability, and respect with future employers. They all know how tough you must work in the sports profession.

Case Study 4

Michael Hitchcock
Director Of Ticket Sales
Los Angels Galaxy

How long have you been at your current position?

A little over 1 year with the Los Angels Galaxy.

What other professional positions have you held?

Clear Channel Communications Radio Sales Account Executive—Richmond VA

DC United—Corporate Sales Executive

Colorado Rapids—Director of Sales/ Sr. Director of Sales & Marketing

LA Galaxy—Director of Sales

How & when did you know you wanted a career in pro sports?

I've always been passionate about sports and knew that my dream job was in sports. I remember hanging out with my friends during my second semester of senior year in college and we were contemplating what we were going to do when we graduated. When my friends asked me what I wanted to do, I grabbed a napkin and a pen and wrote down three words . . . Sales. Marketing. Soccer. At that moment, I knew this was my dream job and set the goal of reaching it. I placed the napkin in my wallet and kept it. Knowing that one day I would reach my goal of working in sports, I accepted a job in radio sales because I could not find a job in sports right out of school. However, two years later I accepted the position of Corporate Sales Executive for DC United. When I accepted the job working with DC United, I finally reached my goal of working in Sports.

How did you "break in"—what was your first job in pro sports?

I was working for Clear Channel Communications in Richmond, Virginia. Selling radio advertising. When DC United and MLS started in 1996, I sold DC United an ad campaign for their inaugural season. I felt like I did a pretty good sales job selling DC United a radio ad in Richmond, Virginia, when they played all of their home games in Washington, D.C. almost two hours away. A year later, after successfully renewing the DC United ad buy, I inquired about sales opportunities with DC United. I actually received my first interview knowing that DC United did not have any sales positions open. However, I figured that I was better off getting to know people in their organization and proving to them that I had all the necessary qualifications to be in sales, even if a position was not currently open. After I interviewed with them, a week or so later a sales position opened up and I was lucky enough to get hired by the flagship franchise in Major League Soccer. If I had never asked for the interview, even though they weren't hiring at the time, I would have never gotten the job when the position opened up unexpectedly.

What sacrifices did you make in order to get into pro sports?

The main sacrifices working in sports have been lack of family time and money . . . Working in sports is the greatest career in the world but the sacrifices are that you work a lot of evenings and weekends which is time taken away from your family. The key to success in sports is to find a balance between career and personal life. This is not always easy. However, when you find that balance it works. Also, for the majority of a person's career in sports you'll make less money than you would in another industry. But it's worth it, because in the end you are doing what you love. You get paid to do things that other people pay money to do, such as attend professional games. But there is still a sacrifice and that must be accepted working in sports. There are always pros with the cons.

What risks did you take?

The main risk that I took was that in order to break into sports, I had to leave an established position where I had developed a solid book of business and accept my dream job where one hundred percent of my time would be spent on establishing new business. I also took a major pay cut in base salary and commissions the first year, because I was starting over again with no established accounts or business. However, in the end it was a calculated risk and one that paid off. Less than three seasons later I was making more money than I could have if I had stayed at my position in radio sales, and less than four years later I was a director of sales with a Major League Soccer franchise. Now, I am doing far better than I could have if I had stayed in radio advertising sales.

What advice would you give individuals who want to pursue a career in professional sports?

I would write down your dream job on a piece of paper, just like I did, and do whatever it takes (within the laws of the land and ethics of the industry) to get that job. Sports is the greatest industry in the world, there is no other industry that I can see myself working in. If I work the rest of my career in the professional sports industry, I'll finish my career a happy man. Anyone who has the drive and passion to be successful in sports can do so.

However, you must work hard and put your mind to being the best you can be. Success in professional sports will not always be easy, but you must be patient to get your breaks. If you stay persistent and work hard, it will pay off and you will have sales success.

Senior VP of Corporate Marketing and Executive Seating, National Basketball Association.

Requested to have name and team affiliation remain anonymous.

How and when did you know you wanted a career in pro sports?

Just prior to entering the professional sports world and joining the team that I work for now, I thought I would remain in college athletics. I didn't think I would end up working for a professional team. I thought I would stay in college sports, perhaps becoming an Athletic Director. I had a pretty good college sports job when I was presented with the opportunity to join a professional team.

How did you "break into sports?" What was your first job in pro sports?

I got a call from the Executive VP of my team asking me if I wanted to apply for the Director of PR position that they had vacant. I had a personal relationship with this particular teams President. It sounded like a great opportunity and I decided to take it. So, my first job was a Director of PR for a professional basketball team.

What sacrifices did you make in order to get into professional sports?

The major sacrifice that I made was spending less time with my family. Professional sports is a very demanding career and one that requires you spend a lot of time at your job. A professional NBA job requires countless hours. We play over 40 games at home each season and that adds up to a lot of nights and weekends at the arena. You have to love your job, because the profession is very intense from a time perspective.

What risks did you take?

I took a pretty significant risk leaving my position in college athletics. I had good security working in college. There is good job security working in athletics because you can gain tenure and there is typically less pressure to perform in college sports. There is a lot more risk working for a professional team. If I failed in pro sports, I would have lost job security. The good news is, my professional sports career has paid off and it ended up being worth the risk.

What advice would you give individuals who want to pursue a career in professional sports?

I would advise anyone looking to land a job in sports to get experience in a particular track and try and stay with it. Whether it be sales, PR, broadcasting, marketing or promotions, decide what you want to pursue and try and get as much experience as possible in that field.

You should also try and intern with teams. This will help you gain experience in a particular field. It will also help you network and develop contacts. I actually made the transition from PR to Sales. Sales is probably your best opportunity to get our career start in professional sports. It has the most entry level positions available and you can learn a lot about the business in sales.

CHAPTER 12

Important Final Thoughts

A Note to Candidates Prior to Accepting a Job

There are several final thoughts to consider before making a decision to work for a professional sports team. You have to know what to expect before entering the professional sports business. As you have learned reading the various case studies, sports is not an easy profession to enter in to. You have to be prepared to invest a lot of time in your career. It is an industry that has a lot to offer and can be very glamorous and rewarding. But it is a tough profession where you must weigh the pros and cons.

For starters, you have to know that when you begin your professional sports career, you will most likely start off not making a lot of money. Other jobs typically pay more than professional sports and you should be prepared to deal with this prior to accepting your first job offer.

I believe there was a time early in my sports career that if I applied for food stamps I probably would have been eligible. When I first started at Bison Baseball, I was listed as a full-time temporary employee and earned a very small weekly salary. I also had the opportunity to earn commissions. However, they were very low percentages on incremental sales.

I also had to pay for parking every day and had no benefits or health insurance. This is an extreme case of a low entry-level salary. However, this is still very common with most teams in the minor leagues. You might have to go through a similar situation until you can prove yourself as you begin your professional sports career.

The good thing about ticket sales is that most of the positions are based on some type of commission compensation plan, which means you can earn additional dollars if you do well. Generally speaking, however, you cannot expect to earn a great deal of money during your first couple of years working in sports.

Most people who work in sports do so for a long time, because they love working in the industry and cannot think of another profession where they would be happy going to work every day. Because of this, many sports executives are willing to work for less money than they could be earning somewhere else.

Another thing you have to consider is that you have to commit a lot of time in order to be successful in sports. Most front office positions require you to work most if not all home games. This means you have to work a lot of evening hours and a lot of weekends. This can be very demanding on your personal time. Major League Baseball employees have to invest the most hours of any sport because they play over 72 games at home each season. Furthermore, because teams are in the public eye, there are countless events, player appearances and team functions that take place outside of game days, which takes even more of your personal time. You must be prepared to deal with this and learn how to juggle your professional sports life and personal life.

The final issue to consider is that you should learn how the team you might work for treats its employees. It is important that you do a little investigative work prior to accepting a job so you know what to expect from the organization. You need to learn about how the team treats all of its employees and most important, how it treats its ticket sales executives in the office.

More and more sports organizations are becoming dependant on proactive ticket sales in order to succeed filling the stands on a consistent basis. This means there is a growing trend toward sales- and marketing-driven organizations. This is a good thing because these sports organizations understand the importance of hiring and retaining quality sales people.

However, many professional sports teams are still in what I like to call the "old school" mentality of conducting business.

They believe that everyone who works for their team is privileged to be able to do so and they treat their front office staff with little respect. They usually also pay less than other sports organizations and turnover within these types of organizations is high. They are teams who have been accustomed to and have been spoiled by a high demand for their product. They have been spoiled by high fan interest, which means they have not had to aggressively sell or market their team.

Many well-established sports organizations have this mentality. They feel that anyone can do the job for their great organization, and if you leave, they'll simply find someone else to fill your shoes.

Because of the more "glamorous" aspects of working for these particular teams, there are a lot of people who want to go to work for them. The New York Yankees are an example of such a team. They are one of the most well-respected sports teams in the world. They have high demand for their product and as a result, they believe everyone wants to be involved with their organization. Furthermore, most players want to play for them, because they pay more money than any other sports team. While most players want to play for them, they are notorious for being one of the most difficult sports teams to work for as a front office employee. They treat their employees poorly and pay the lowest of most sports teams. They feel that people are privileged to work for them and do not appreciate their employees. Except, of course, if you are fortunate enough to be the general manager, or those that work on the team side. They are all paid very well. The New York Yankees general manager, for example, is paid a contract worth millions of dollars. Meanwhile, the entry-level PR person is paid in the low $20,000 range. The Yankees are a very successful organization, so they must be doing a lot of things right. However, I would argue that if they treated their employees a little better than they do, and paid them more than they do, they would have even more success.

You should be aware that these sports organizations exist and you should make your own decision as to whether or not you want to work in that type of environment. I personally would have a difficult time working for one of these teams for any length of time. However, to get your career started in sports you might have to take an opportunity with a team that pays lower than others and treats its employees with less respect. Times are changing in a positive direction, since more teams are becoming dependent on sales and marketing; however, things need to continue to improve.

The other type of sales environment of which to be leery are the teams that take a "boiler-room" approach to sales. Some teams hire up to twenty to thirty sales reps, provide little sales training, and then set them loose to fend for themselves. I call this the "here's your desk and phone, now go sell" sales recruiting approach. These types of teams often set extremely aggressive sales targets and pay very low, which results in only a small percentage of the sales reps staying with the team for any length of time.

These types of environments make it difficult to have consistent long-term sales success because they have little regard for sales and will not invest in their salespeople. You can get good entry-level experience, but it might be difficult to stay with these teams for any length of time.

These types of sales environments also make it difficult to foster teamwork and develop a long-term healthy business environment. Instead, it breeds a cutthroat "every person for themselves" type of sales environment, which makes it difficult to have sales success. To achieve sales success, teamwork is critical.

During the interviewing process, you should ask such questions as the type of training that the team provides, the upward mobility opportunities that exist, the average years of experience the sales staff has, and how long the staff has been there. This will help you determine what type of sales environment the team has.

I have found the boiler-room–type sales environment to be popular in the NBA. One professional NBA franchise that I interviewed with, as an example, told me that they typically hired fifteen sales reps at the beginning of each season, but only had room for ten full-time reps. Their intention was to cut five of the reps after a three-month sales "audition" based on sales results.

At the time I interviewed for this position, I had over three years of professional sales experience. They were not willing to give me any type of consideration for the fact that I had this experience. They still wanted me to go into the program and fight for a position with all of the other reps they planned on hiring.

I certainly understood this team's perspective and hiring practices, however, I didn't agree with their decision to treat me like everyone else. They should have seen that I had over three seasons of successful ticket sales with two different teams and made an exception in my case. Recruiting good salespeople is not an easy task and I would have been a good gamble for them to hire. As a result of their decision to put me in the pool with all other sales candidates, I did not accept their offer.

I feel teams that hire large boiler-room sales staffs take the lazy way out when trying to build and recruit a solid ticket sales team. They decide to hire masses in hopes of keeping a handful of successful reps. By hiring a large number of sales reps, they are bound to find a few who will be successful. I came across an article recently in the *Sports Business Journal*, "Panthers beef up sales staff despite labor uncertainty." The article read, "The Club plans on bringing in an additional 20 sales people over the next few months, in addition to 25 new hires they recently made. Half of the additional sales people are out of college and do not receive benefits."

While it is fantastic the Panthers are looking to hire more salespeople, I would be leery of their intentions by hiring 20 people. Especially since they will not be paying benefits. My bet is that they are going to only keep a select few for the long term. Instead, they would be better off hiring 10 sales professionals, and taking the time to recruit, hire and train the best people they can find.

I believe this would be a better approach; however, it would require more time in order to screen, interview, and hire top-level candidates who have the greatest chance for sales success. Because it takes more time and is tougher to do, many teams do not do it.

You must be alerted to the obstacles just discussed when looking to land a job with a professional sports team. Some teams offer low-paying job, treat their employees poorly, or have a boiler-room sales operation—you must understand these situations exist in the sports world. You might have to deal with all three undesirable aspects when you accept your first job. I have been subject to all of them, however, I found ways to overcome them.

I hope the tide is changing and that more and more teams are thinking about how they pay and treat their employees. They also should develop ways to retain their most productive employees. In the end, a team is only as good as the players who play the game, but also as good as the people who work in the front offices. Most successful companies, especially in the service industry, will tell you that human resources are their most important resources. Professional sports teams are no different than other companies, therefore their human resources are important for success.

Note to Team Presidents, General Managers, Stadiums, and Owners

I would like to take this forum to say a few words to those in sports who make decisions about how they pay and treat their front office employees. Although there is a changing attitude within professional sports, there are still too many sports teams that are still operating in the "old school" mentality of conducting sports business. They have been spoiled by high demand for their products at certain times, and have also become greedy be receiving millions of dollars in television money. Therefore, they conduct business with a certain amount of arrogance and lose site of the fact that paying fans are indeed their customers. There are also way too many sports stadiums and venues still operating in this manner as well.

In my opinion, they are the teams and the sports venues that are bringing the sports world down and contributing to all of the factors that are adding to the decline in attendance. These types of teams run the risk of losing many talented professionals to other industries as well as to other teams. I have seen many very talented people leave professional sports, to the detriment of the teams they leave behind due to unfair pay and treatment.

Once again, most people who work in sports know they can probably make more money elsewhere and are willing to accept this situation. However, there are many situations where what the employee puts into the organization and what they feel they get out becomes inequitable. After a certain amount of time, frustration builds up and the employee leaves. Constant turnover within a sports team is not good for a team's long-term success. This is another contributing factor as to why many teams are losing fans.

I don't think many general managers, team presidents, or owners really know what is happening in the marketplace. I believe many of them are out of touch with what is happening on the front lines of trying to attract customers. Too many of them are simply focused on the team and the product on the field. They are surrounded by people who love their teams, whether it be people in the media, other executives working with other teams, or a few hundred fans who e-mail them and want to talk to them all the time.

Meanwhile, while they are surrounded by the bubble of everything that goes on with the team, their teams are losing fans every day and if attitudes don't change in sports, I am afraid professional sports are in jeopardy of losing many more fans for years to come.

If the sports industry is not careful, this can make the financial climate difficult for years to come as well. Teams, franchises, and perhaps even entire leagues might end up folding or shutting down operations. Things might be worse than what many people think. Plus, if most stadiums and venues continue to run their stadiums like military camps, instead of fan-friendly places where customers feel welcome, the problem will worsen.

I believe more and more teams must begin to run their business like every other business. Professional sports are in the leisure entertainment business. Competition for the entertainment dollar is growing, and in the end sports teams are no different than any other type of business in this category. However, many sports teams do not run like other businesses. I often think to myself that if some of the other companies that I worked for ran like many professional sports teams do, those other businesses would quickly become bankrupt. It also doesn't help that many people in professional sports have never worked outside of the industry. Things are much different in other places of business where companies are fighting for the dollar every day.

However, many professional sports teams have been spoiled by a strong demand for their product. As a result of this strong demand, they typically only focus on the team side of the business, building winning teams, paying high salaries to star players, coaches and general managers. However, many things that were taken for granted are now changing and cannot be taken for granted any longer.

Unfortunately, many teams have never really learned how to properly sell and market their product. They relied on simple traditional marketing and advertising campaigns and sat back and watched people buy their product. Some teams never had to go out into the marketplace and proactively sell.

As a result, this has affected the way many teams hire and treat their employees. If you look at most successful companies in any industry, they will tell you that human resources are the most important aspect of their business. I don't believe many professional sports teams feel the same way.

Most professional sports team owners are only concerned about two things, winning and star players. They feel if you win or have star players, people will come. Winning strokes the owners' egos and makes them feel good about owning a team. Nothing makes many owners happier than hoisting the championship trophy high on national television. No one can argue also about the impact of star players on a team. Many star players such as Larry Bird, Michael Jordon, Wayne Gretsky, Freddy Adu, and Tiger Woods have made their respective sports into the popular products that they are today. Unfortunately, these type of players are far and few between, and true super star athletes do not come around everyday.

Of course, the game as well as the players are the most important thing and the reason most people love sports. Because without them there would be no teams. The game being played is the most exciting part of sports, but is not the only part of it.

Because most owners care only about the team, this is where they spend all of their money. They spend it on players, coaches, team staff, and general managers, all in order to help the team win. What often gets ignored is the behind-the-scenes business aspects of sports. As a result, the front-office people sometimes are the ones who get the least amount of recognition, earn the least amount of money, and are treated with the least amount of respect.

Most of the time, the front-office people are the ones doing all of the "dirty" work, the non-glamorous behind the scenes stuff. They put in the most hours and sweat equity, and truly help the team be successful off the field. More effort and time are put in by front-office staff than most players and top level executives recognize. As the sports business becomes tougher and tougher where fighting for the dollar becomes a harder challenge, owners will need to focus more on recruiting and retaining quality sports business executives. Not only executives who can help them win a championships, but executives who can help sell and market their teams and drive in revenue, while building strong business relationships

Therefore, my note to team owners is simple. Treat your office employees with more respect, pay them what they are worth, and find ways to retain the services of your best employees because good employees are hard to find. Everyone involved with the organization impacts how the general public thinks about a team.

I am not suggesting that the front-office staff should get paid in line with the star players on the team or the General Mangers. However, I am suggesting some front-office staff might be more valuable than the credit for which they are given. It still appears there is still a huge disparity within a team's front office and what the people involved with the team are being paid versus what the sales and marketing executives are being paid.

Winning teams will drive in revenue to a team, but in the long run, this is not nearly as much money as what the sales and marketing people can bring in by building solid business relationships.

It might not always be a financial boost that is needed either; it might be simple signs of appreciation that is needed to retain top executives. Keeping and maintaining quality people will help teams succeed. High-staff turnover can be costly to the team, more costly than the small things to retain top employees.

For example, when I worked at Bison Baseball, I was fortunate enough to work with a great, young ambitious sales staff. However, I do not believe that management truly recognized and appreciated how good a sales staff they had. As a result, they lost everyone from this great staff. I believe it cost them more money in the long run by losing talented people, than it would have cost to retain them.

They failed to do little things to keep this great sales team intact. For starters, compensation was extremely low with salaries lower than the industry standards.

They could have simply raised everyone's salaries by $2,000 to $3,000 and many of us would have stayed around a lot longer. Five reps × $3,000 in base salary equals $15,000 dollars in total additional salary. In the grand scheme of their business, $15,000 is not all that significant. They would have easily sold $15,000 of additional tickets to offset this investment in their salespeople due to the talent level on that sales team. Furthermore, training and recruiting new employees is a very costly proposition. It is difficult to put an exact dollar figure on the cost; however, interviewing, recruiting and training a new salesperson is costly. Professional recruiters typically ask for 20 percent of a candidate's year-one salary. Plus, typically a solid year of sales experience is needed for a new sales rep to build solid relationships and produce significant revenue. A first year ticket sales rep will never make more money than a sales rep with one or more years experience.

However, even if the Bisons couldn't justify $3,000 more in base salary per rep, they could have done little thing to keep the sales team happy. Simple things such as passing out complementary tickets to other area sporting events, paying for staff meals, offering free team merchandise, or simple recognitions and rewards for good sales performance might have made a difference. Simple things such as these would not have cost management a lot of money but would have kept the sales team happy and loyal.

Because of lack of incentives, many talented individuals left the organization before they reached their potential. As a result, the organization lost not only a number of new sales opportunities, but they also lost a lot of repeat business. Many reps had established great relationships with their clients and many clients had bought because of their reps. Many of these relationships ended when the reps left the organization.

The good news is that there are many new sports owners who are starting to care about the business side of sports business and are beginning to recruit true professionals. They also understand they need to pay more in line with industry standards in order to recruit and retain employees who can drive revenue. I have been fortunate enough to work for two Major League Soccer teams who have treated me fairly and equitable given their constraints. They truly value and appreciate what sales and marketing executives can bring to the table.

However, there is still a large disparity in the sports world between the team side of the business and the sales and marketing side of the business. It always amazes me how much an owner is willing to pay a general manager or player, offering contracts worth millions of dollars, but will complain about a $2,000 raise for a ticket sales rep. Or, they will have no problem gearing up the players, coaching staff and everyone on the team side of the business with team merchandise, however they won't give a team sweatshirt to people in the front office. This mentality is something that I cannot understand and is something that will hopefully change in the future.

Last Words

By reading this book you should have gained a new appreciation for ticket sales as a profession in the sports industry. It is a profession that gets little recognition and credit, however, it is the backbone of many sports teams and produces a large percentage of teams' revenue. It is the primary revenue stream for teams without television contracts and deserves more recognition.

The tips contained in this book will help you lead a successful career in ticket sales and hopefully you will find this career to be as fulfilling as I have found. Remember, the sky is truly the limit and if you set your mind to it, you can accomplish anything you want in your sports career.

Furthermore, it is my intention that other executives in the sports business will read this book and gain a new appreciation for ticket sales. I want people who run stadiums to look at ticket sales reps as well as fans differently than they do now, and re-examine how they run their stadiums. Stadium operators need to treat fans and employees more like paying customers and less like people intruding upon their sacred grounds.

Many PR directors, marketing directors, sponsorship directors, team administrators, coaches, and general managers lack knowledge and respect for ticket salespeople. I hope that they will look at ticket sales in a different light than they did prior to reading this book. If a few other sports executives look at ticket sales differently than they previously did, I have accomplished something by writing this book.

Please visit my Web site at www.breakintosports.com and feel free to send me an e-mail about any sports business topic you wish to discuss. I welcome your comments and feedback because I hope to make changes to future editions and your comments will help.

I wish you all the best in your professional sports career. I hope you break into sports through ticket sales, reach your goals, dreams, and desires. *Carpe Diem*, go for it—METAL—\M/!!!

Final Acknowledgments

There are many people in my professional as well as private life that I would like to thank. All have contributed in some way to my current ticket sales success, which has led me to be in a position where I am able to write this book. Therefore, I would like to recognize them here.

I would like to thank Richard Moldenhauer and Cordes Williams at Moldenhouer and Associates in Buffalo, New York. They took a chance and hired me out of college, when most people wouldn't. Cordes Williams mentored me and provided my first professional sales training. It was their sales training that helped me succeed in sports sales.

I would like to thank Warren Z. Rubin, Peter Sinagra and Mike Harloff from my Bison Baseball days. Warren hired me into the Direct Marketing Department of Bison Baseball and taught me a great deal about sports telemarketing. He hired and trained the first successful telemarketing department of Bison Baseball. Peter Sinagra was the Sales Director and had a great influence on my professional sports sales career. I still quote today many of the things Peter said during our numerous sales meetings and respect his leadership. Mike Harloff ended up working with me at DC United and not only did we sell a ton of tickets working together, we became best friends.

I would like to thank Fred Matthes and Susan O'Malley from my days at the Washington Bullets. Fred hired me as a telemarketing rep and then promoted me into a full time sales position. He also hired me when he took the Director of Sales position at DC United. I owe a lot to Fred for helping me get my pro sports career start in the Washington D.C. area. Susan O'Malley was a great team President and treated all of her employees, including me, fairly.

I would like to thank Kevin Payne, Stephen Zack, Betty D'Anjollel and the rest of the DC United staff. Kevin had the vision to hire successful people on and off the field and he helped DC United win three championships. This made all of our jobs much easier.

Betty D'Anjollel was the Executive VP of DC United and I have a ton of respect and admiration for her. While she was often very tough, she was also fair and helped build a great winning organization. Stephen Zack took over for Betty when she left DC United and, thanks to his hard work, our organization did not miss a beat.

I would also like to recognize the rest of the DC United staff. They treated me like I was part of a second family. Michael Hitchcock, Dan Giffin, Chris Keeney, Drew Young, Mike Harloff,

Bien Martinez, Bruce Bundrandt, Kwame Bryant, Josh Goodstadt, Jason Hynd, Scott Mears, Carl Miklans, Frank Moore, Skip Krueger, Jamie O'Conner, Dennis Lee, Ray Trifari, Catherine Marquette, Kimberly Lane, Michael Kammarman, Rick Lawes, Beau Wright, Charles Raycraft, Bruce Arena, Bob Bradley, Dave Sarachan and Thomas Rongen.

I would like to thank my current team at the MetroStars. Special thanks to John Guppy and Nick Sakeiwicz for bringing me to the MetroStars. They convinced me to leave a place that I loved in order to further my professional sales career. So far the move has paid off. I would also like to thank Chris Canetti who is one of the best Marketing guys in the business. I have learned a great deal working with this current executive team and have become a better sales manager as a result.

I would also like to thank my current ticket sales team. In 2003 we worked hard to earn the 2003 MLS Ticket Sales Team of the Year award. They all did a great job and we deserved the league recognition. Tony Alessandra, Earl Alcalde, James Martin, Patrick Beattie, Maya Mallan, Mike Mondello, Steve Samaggaio, and Mike Quarino.

Special thanks as well to all the people who helped me with the case studies chapter. Drew Young, Chris Schiller, Marc Steir, Michael Hitchcock and my NBA contact. Thanks to Sue Mukoda, who worked with me on the editing stages. I also need to thank Mark Risenburg whose book *Stop Whining and Start Winning* inspired me to write my own book. Plus, special thanks goes to Metal Mike Chlassiak. He brought out the creative spirit in me and inspired me to create something that was my own.

Finally, I would like to thank some people in my personal life who helped me reach my goals. They have all given me a great deal support and encouraged me to finish writing this book, when many time I had doubts whether or not it was worth it. I would like to thank my parents, Mike and Ceil Washo for raising me and giving me the opportunities to lead a successful professional life. They put me through college and taught me leadership skills that help me every day.

I would also like to thank my brothers Jeff, Keith and Dave who all support me and give different advice at different times. Each of them is very important to me and all have helped in many aspects of my life.

I would also like to thank my wife Wendy who helped me with the editing stages of this book. She gave me a ton of support and guidance when I was writing this and has been a great wife and is a great Mom as well. Finally I would like to thank many of my friends for being such great friends. I cannot list them all here, but they know who they are!

Finally, this book is dedicated to my grandfathers John Malitsky and Wassil Washo, my grandmothers Sophie Malitsky and Helen Washo. Last but not least, I dedicate this book to my daughter, Sophie Anne Washo.

Special thanks to all!

Order Form

Break Into Sports Through Ticket Sales

This book makes the perfect gift for anyone interested in professional sports. To order additional copies, simply tear out this order form and send it to the address listed below. Thank you again for purchasing this book.

Name: _____

Address: _____

City: _____ State: _____ Zip: _____

Phone: _____

E-mail: _____

Special re-order price: $15.95   (Regular price $19.95)

# of Copies _____ × $15.95   = _____

NJ State Tax × 6%   = _____

Shipping   = $5

Total   = _____

Make checks payable to MMW Marketing

Send Checks to: MMW Marketing
PO Box 1670
Rutherford, NJ 07070

mmwasho@aol.com

Thank you!
Mark Washo

Order Form

Break Into Sports
Through Ticket Sales

This book makes the perfect gift for anyone interested in professional sports. To order additional copies, simply tear out this order form and send it to the address listed below. Thank you again for purchasing this book.

Name: _____

Address: _____

City: _____ State: _____ Zip: _____

Phone: _____

E-mail: _____

Special re-order price: $15.95   (Regular price $19.95)

# of Copies ____ × $15.95   = _____

NJ State Tax × 6%   = _____

Shipping   = $5

Total   = _____

Make checks payable to MMW Marketing

Send Checks to: MMW Marketing
PO Box 1670
Rutherford, NJ 07070

mmwasho@aol.com

Thank you!
Mark Washo